7
B.
Fin
in

L

?

E

2

28 M

WITH THE
DUBLIN BRIGADE

WITH THE
DUBLIN BRIGADE

Espionage and Assassination
with Michael Collins' Intelligence Unit

CHARLES DALTON

MERCIER PRESS
IRISH PUBLISHER – IRISH STORY

MERCIER PRESS

Cork

www.mercierpress.ie

© Estate of Charles Dalton, 2014

© Foreword: Liz Gillis, 2014

ISBN: 978 1 78117 224 7

10 9 8 7 6 5 4 3 2 1

A CIP record for this title is available from the British Library

Printed and bound in the EU.

CONTENTS

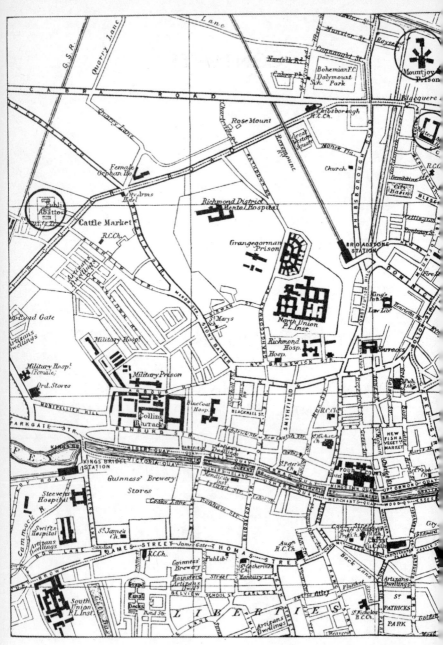

MAP OF CENTRAL DUBLIN WITH PLACES MENTIONED
IN THE STORY MARKED WITH CIRCLES

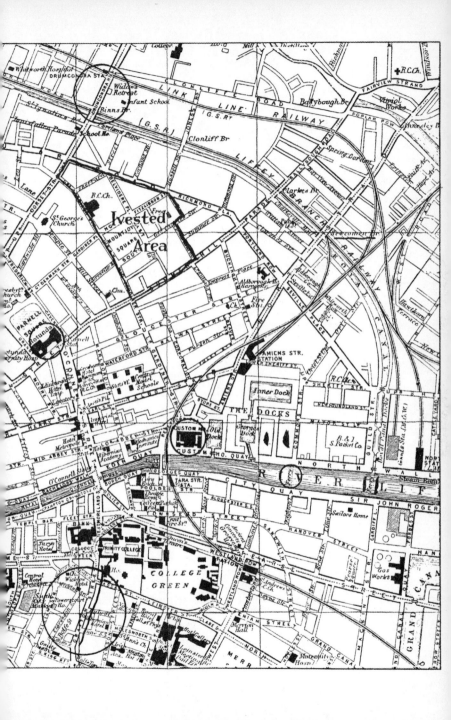

FOREWORD

With the Dublin Brigade tells the story of one man's role in the Irish War of Independence. First published in 1929, the author, Charles Dalton, was but a young man, only twenty-six years old, when he decided to write about his experiences during the conflict that resulted in Ireland winning independence, although not full independence, from Great Britain.

Dalton was born in January 1903 to James Francis Dalton, a staunch supporter and advocate of Home Rule, and his wife Katherine. He was the third of six children. The family had lived in America for some time, where Charles' two older brothers Martin and Emmet were born, but then returned to Dublin where the next four children, Charles, Eileen, Brendan and Dermot (Pat) arrived. Their early family life was stable and happy, but as with so many young men and women of that generation, events far out of their control would affect them in ways that they could never imagine.

And so begin the first pages of Dalton's story.

Immediately we are introduced to thirteen-year-old Charles' description of the event that would have such a profound effect on him – the 1916 Easter Rising. Although his older brother Emmet was fighting for the British Army in the First World War, Charles makes no mention of that conflict, a conflict that had an impact on so many people the world over. To him the men and women who made a stand during that week in April 1916 were his heroes and in that moment, like so many of his generation at that time, Charles decided that if a future opportunity arose, he, too, would play his part in helping to free Ireland.

The young men and women who had witnessed the aftermath of the Easter Rising were determined that when they would fight again it would be on their terms. Knowing that they were outnumbered both in manpower and weaponry, they used every advantage at their disposal to attack and undermine the crown forces. Countless books have been written by participants of the Rising, the War of Independence and the Civil War, and these accounts give an invaluable insight into that period of our turbulent history. However, *With the Dublin Brigade* differs somewhat to the other publications, in that it not only describes how the War of Independence was actually fought in Dublin, but, more importantly, it also describes the methods used by the Republicans in the intelligence war against the crown forces.

The Volunteers, or Irish Republican Army (IRA) as they were to become known from 1919, fought their war on three levels – 1) undermining the civil administration, 2) physical attacks and 3) intelligence. This three-pronged assault was to be very effective, and the IRA intelligence units around the country, but especially in Dublin and Cork, were vital to this new type of warfare. The authorities never expected to be attacked through their own intelligence system – a system which had been used again and again to great effect against previous attempts by the Irish to obtain their freedom. And this is where Charles Dalton's story is unique. Not only was it written just eight years after hostilities between Great Britain and Ireland ceased but, more importantly, it is a first-hand account of how the intelligence war was fought by young men and women who, although putting themselves in great danger, carried on regardless in order to free their country. The very nature of their work required the utmost secrecy but, through Charles' story, we catch a glimpse of what it was like to participate in such activities.

His story reads like a film script, the memories of such momentous events in his life still fresh in his mind. And in those first few chapters we see him grow up very quickly.

In December 1917, aged just fourteen, Charles officially became a member of the Volunteers, joining F Company, 2nd Battalion, Dublin Brigade. His description of his first 'official job' is full of excitement, even though he was only helping in the cleaning and removal of pigs' carcasses to be cured by local factories. He wrote, '*Dramatic accounts of this incident appeared in the newspapers. It gave me a feeling of elation to receive this public recognition of what was my first job.*'

His descriptions of events are at times funny, for example dressing in his father's clothes to make himself look older. We see his rise through the ranks of the IRA, firstly assisting the Squad and then as a member of Michael Collins' Intelligence Unit, and we are soon introduced to those men who would become some of his closest friends. Through Dalton we hear their stories too. All of them he held in the highest regard and when telling of those who did not survive the conflict he does not shy away from expressing how their deaths affected him, especially that of Dick McKee, OC Dublin Brigade, in the aftermath of Bloody Sunday, 1920.

Surprisingly, Dalton goes into great detail about the build-up to the events of Bloody Sunday. As an active participant in the shootings he gives a first-hand account of the events, not only of the shootings themselves, but of how it felt to actually carry out the shooting of the British agents, not in battle, but in their residences. He writes: '*I was wrought up, thinking of what we had to do the next morning, and I could feel the other men were the same ... Outwardly we were calm and collected, even jesting with each other. But inwardly I felt that the others were as I was –*

palpitating with anxiety.' Of the aftermath he wrote: '*The sights and sounds of that morning were to be with me for many days and nights …*'

As the story progresses we see the effect the war had on its participants: '*We slept lightly, waking often with a start to hear a lorry pulling up outside … Even in our slumbers, the sense of danger was always near us.*'

One very important point to remember is that this book was written long before any attempts were made to record the stories of those involved in the revolutionary movement. Thankfully, through the work of Ernie O'Malley and later the Bureau of Military History, these stories *were* recorded, but they were not in the public domain until recently. With the release of the BMH Witness Statements online and the recent publication of some of the O'Malley notebooks we are finally getting to see the real people behind the events, those men and women who gave so much for the freedom of this country.

Charles Dalton himself made a witness statement for the Bureau in 1950, twenty-one years after *With the Dublin Brigade* was published. His statement differs slightly in detail to the book, for example a name here and there. One possibility for these differences is that he was protecting the real identity of those who helped or gave information – after all the book was written only nine years after the events on Bloody Sunday. Where it differs *most* is in the use of language. The twenty-six-year-old Charles Dalton has now matured – the facts are presented just like they are in the book, but he is older. Here we meet the now forty-seven-year-old Charles Dalton, husband, father, civilian – a wiser and certainly more reflective man.

To conclude, I want to draw attention to one very important statement in the original introduction to the book: *'The Irish struggle of 1916–1921 was not and is not yet understood by those who did not take part in it or sympathize with it.'* This is as true today as it was in 1929.

This new edition of *With the Dublin Brigade* is a vital publication and a welcome addition to the many personal recollections published over the years. Through this book and indeed any of the other accounts, be they books, diaries or letters written by those men and women who were involved, and now through their witness statements, we can at last gain an insight, no matter how small, into what their experiences were, what their hopes were and what motivated them to do what they felt they had to do, turning ordinary people into extraordinary men and women.

And whether we agree or disagree with them, at least we should now begin to see them as real people.

LIZ GILLIS

INTRODUCTION

The Irish struggle of 1916–1921 was not and is not yet understood by those who did not take part in it or sympathize with it. The episodes described in this book are of novel and dramatic interest, and the story told may serve to throw light on the nature of the struggle, and on the startling changes which marked its end.

'We have got murder by the throat,' said Mr Lloyd George, the British Prime Minister, on 9th October 1920. He 'hoped for good results from maintaining the pressure' which the British armed forces were exerting in Ireland. He 'could not permit the country to be debased into a condition of complete anarchy where a small body of assassins, a real murder gang, were dominating the country and terrorizing it'. 'It is,' he exclaimed, 'a sham and a fraud, the whole of this nationality.' 'Undoubtedly you must restore order there by methods very stern.' 'It is essential in the interests of Ireland that that gang should be broken up, and unless I am mistaken, we shall do it.'

The so-called reprisals – acts of terrorism and sabotage – by the British armed forces were casually mentioned by Mr Lloyd George as 'some severe hitting back by the gallant men who are doing their duty in Ireland'.

To his fellow-banqueters at the London Guildhall in the following month Mr Lloyd George spoke lightly of Ireland as 'one disturbed corner of the Empire'. He announced that 'the police were getting the right men', without troubling to explain who 'the police' were, what 'getting' meant, or in what sense they were 'the right men'.

What was the British law and order in Ireland which Mr Lloyd George was enforcing? The London *Times* wrote on 15th November 1920: 'Persistence in the present method of Irish Government will, we are satisfied, be proved utterly irreconcilable with the ideals of this Christian country.'

Who was terrorizing Ireland and debasing it into a condition of anarchy? Was it overlooked by Mr Lloyd George that while the British administration was deteriorating into a licensed lawlessness, the Irish people were successfully engaged in building up their own self-government?

Historians are still in want of authentic material to explain the turning point when the British Government at last decided that they must seek for peace. At first they set about negotiations secretly through intermediaries, restricting the matters on which they were willing to confer. They let it be known that they would give safe conducts to any accredited Irish negotiators whose names were not upon their 'black list' as criminals, and, therefore, outside the pale, and that they would give notice in advance of such names. They would exclude from any terms of peace 'persons reasonably suspected of murder'.

Many of the soldiers of the Irish Republican Army had already been hanged. One Irish officer lay in Mountjoy Jail under sentence of death. But there were at least three men whom the British had not succeeded in capturing (the 'right men' whom Mr Lloyd George was still hoping to 'get'), whom it was known the British Government meant as 'persons reasonably suspected of murder' – Cathal Brugha, the Minister of Defence, Richard Mulcahy, the Chief of Staff, and Michael Collins, the Minister for Finance and Chief Intelligence Officer, who was being hunted with the price of £10,000 on his head.

Dáil Éireann (the Irish Parliament) had been declared an 'illegal assembly'. Thirty-six of its members were in penal servitude or otherwise imprisoned or interned. These included Arthur Griffith, who was acting President while President de Valera was in America, and who later headed the Irish plenipotentiaries in London. They also included Seán MacEoin, who had been tried by court martial and sentenced to death. As a General of the Irish Army he was afterwards to take over from the English the stronghold of Athlone. Another member, Robert Barton, was undergoing penal servitude in an English prison, and on his release was chosen as one of the Irish plenipotentiaries.

President de Valera, who had been rescued in 1919 from

Lincoln Gaol by Michael Collins, had recently returned from America. On the eve of the Truce he was arrested, but was promptly released, without reason given, obviously with a view to the possibility of negotiations.

Michael Collins himself was alive and free, but not by the grace of the British Government. How he had eluded the hounds who were continually on his track, is one of the miracles of history. The British were aware that Michael Collins dominated and directed the whole movement. His name was the blackest on the British list. He was the supreme outlaw.

But the climax of the long struggle had already been reached. Events had acquired a momentum which was hurrying them to an inevitable conclusion.

In June 1921, the British Government publicly proposed a conference with the Irish leaders. The previous attempts to impose restrictions on the conference were abandoned. The 'black list' was thrown into the wastepaper basket. In his letter of 24th June 1921 to President de Valera, Mr Lloyd George proposed that he should attend a conference in London 'to explore to the utmost the possibility of a settlement', and he invited him 'to bring with him for the purpose any colleagues whom he might select'.

Terms of Truce were arranged between military officers on both sides on 9th July 1921.

A Peace Conference followed. The right of Ireland

as a nation under arms to decide its own destiny was acknowledged. By the Treaty of Peace made between the two nations and afterwards ratified by the British Parliament at Westminster and by Dáil Éireann in Dublin, the Irish Government, deriving its authority from the Irish people and controlling its own army and civil administration, was acknowledged by England and the other nations of the world.

Michael Collins, with Arthur Griffith, was one of the Irish plenipotentiaries, and his was one of the signatures to the Treaty. On the 16th January 1922, as head of the Provisional Government, he took over from Lord Fitzalan the historic Dublin Castle, from which for seven centuries the British had sought to exercise dominion over Ireland.

The wheel of destiny, moved by forces which the historian must appraise, had come full circle. The British Government had completed their volte-face.

In December 1922, a year later, Mr Lloyd George, writing a description of the Peace Conference, said:

> Opposite to me sat a dark, short but sturdy figure, with the face of a thinker. That was Mr Arthur Griffith … quiet to the point of gentleness, reserved almost to the point of appearing saturnine. A man of laconic utterance … But we found in our few weeks' acquaintance that his 'yea' was 'yea,' and his 'nay' meant 'nay.' By his side sat a handsome young

Irishman. No one could mistake his nationality. He was Irish through and through. Vivacious, buoyant, highly strung, gay, impulsive, but passing readily from gaiety to grimness and back again to gaiety, full of fascination and charm – but also of dangerous fire. That was Michael Collins, one of the most courageous leaders ever produced by a valiant race.

What were the forces which brought one of the most powerful nations in history to recant its indictments and to acknowledge as a nation on an equality with itself, a country which it had long sought to treat as conquered, and to incorporate as a province? Who were the men who brought it about, what were the aims and methods of the leaders, and the men who followed them?

As yet many essential details have remained hidden in mystery, known only to the actors themselves. There had been months and years of endurance, days and nights of agony, yet illumined by a spirit of exultant faith and the joys of comradeship. One or two frank, unadorned pictures by the men who in the humbler positions played an essential part will tell more than any second-hand history, and will enable persons and events to stand out in their truth. This story by a young Irish soldier who took part in the decisive stage of the struggle must appeal to readers who are interested in human character, or appreciate drama, or are concerned with the history of nations. But for those who are not well acquainted with the history of Ireland leading up to and including the period covered by this memoir, the following summary may serve as a prologue.

The Irish people as a nation had never acquiesced in the British occupation. They were never willing citizens of the United Kingdom.

But for half a century before 1916 Ireland's claim to nationality had been represented chiefly by the Irish Parliamentary Party. Its members sat as Ireland's representatives in the British House of Commons. Though always in a minority there, they claimed that by holding the balance of power they would some day be able to force an English Government to restore the Parliament in Dublin, which had been abolished in 1800 by the Act of Union. In the meanwhile, they assisted legislation, especially Land Acts, with a view to ameliorating conditions in Ireland.

But there were always Irishmen who had no such faith in the British Parliament, in its ability to govern Ireland according to Irish ideas, in its right to determine Ireland's destiny, or in its will to listen to the national demand. Consequently, there had been in nearly every generation an armed revolt. Few in numbers, and with inadequate arms (which had to be procured secretly), the insurgents were always defeated. But when they had been hanged, imprisoned, or transported, they became the heroes and martyrs of Ireland, and the faith for which they had suffered remained alive in the imagination of the people.

In 1858, a secret society, the Irish Republican Brotherhood, better known as the Fenians, was founded by James Stephens. The Brotherhood was a militant organization which inherited the ideas of John Mitchell, an earlier patriot-convict. He had asserted that the physical force argument was the only one to which England had ever listened in her relations with Ireland. Any alleviations of the miseries of the Irish under English rule had come only after violence or preparation for violence. The Fenians, further, shared his view that unless a people from time to time asserted its right to freedom by force of arms it surrendered its claim to be a nation.

The existence of the Irish Republican Brotherhood was in due course discovered by the police (the Royal Irish Constabulary, who were trained to act as political detectives), and Stephens and most of the Executive Council, including the writer and patriot, O'Donovan Rossa, were arrested and sentenced to long terms of penal servitude.

The Fenian policy was embodied in the phrase 'England's difficulty is Ireland's opportunity'. The organization survived the arrests of 1865 and was kept in being secretly all through the era of the Irish Parliamentary Party. It was part of its policy that there should be at all times at least a few men who would be prepared to strike a blow for Irish independence whenever a suitable opportunity arose.

In the United States there was a branch of the Brotherhood. It was known there as the Clan-na-Gael. Its leader was John Devoy, who had been arrested with the other Fenians, and who had emigrated to America after serving a long sentence in an English penal prison. Through John Devoy, the Clan-na-Gael was in close touch with the parent organization at home and kept it supplied with funds for every kind of genuine patriotic purpose.

In Ireland the Brotherhood was strengthened by the release in 1909 of another Fenian, an old comrade of Devoy's – Tom Clarke. Clarke had spent twenty years in penal servitude in England, and, on his release, he took a small tobacconist's shop in Parnell Street, Dublin. There he administered the oath of the Brotherhood to a number of ardent young men who found no inspiration in the policy of the parliamentarians.

Besides this secret militant organization there was another with similar aims – the liberation of Ireland from the domination of England – but which looked to other methods to achieve them. This was the Sinn Féin organization founded by Arthur Griffith. In his weekly paper, *The United Irishman* (afterwards *Nationality*), Griffith wrote that Ireland could only be freed by the determined action of Irishmen themselves. He pointed to the example of Hungary and the means by which it was liberated from the grip of Austria. He preached passive resistance to English rule and an active social constructive policy in Ireland, by which the people should gradually take their political affairs into their own hands and squeeze out the British administration. Griffith was not opposed to the use of physical force (when it found its place afterwards in defending Dáil Éireann and in resisting the campaign of the Black and Tans, he supported every action of the Irish Republican Army), but he saw no hope of his people ever being strong enough to free their country by a military victory.

The men who formed these two organizations were in numbers insignificant, but in brain and character they were by no means so. Tom Clarke was a man of burning patriotic faith and unquenchable courage, and his private influence was enormous. He was looked up to by the men who gathered round him as the bearer of the traditional torch of Irish freedom out of the heroic days of the past. Amongst others, he inspired a young man of great charm of personality – Seán MacDermott, who, though in delicate health, tramped through the country towns and villages, enrolling small groups of young patriots into the Brotherhood.

Arthur Griffith's powerful mind and indomitable character were also bound to draw to him men of force and sincerity. Devoted to his faith, he was content to preach in poverty and obscurity, confident that if the time ever came when his policy could be put into practice, Ireland would be free.

There were two other organizations, which, though non-political, fostered the spirit of patriotism and helped to produce the great national revival of later years. They were the Gaelic League and the Gaelic Athletic Association. The Gaelic League was founded to revive the national language and the Gaelic Athletic Association for the preservation of Gaelic sport. Many of the men of the Irish Republican Brotherhood were members also of one or both of these organizations, and were often recruited from them. There were also the Fianna, a Republican organization of youths recruited from the Dublin streets by Countess Markiewicz, and drilled and trained by her to act as scouts and carry despatches; and Cumann na mBan, the women's branch of the military organization.

This was the position in Ireland when, at last, in 1914, the efforts of the Irish Parliamentary Party were so far rewarded that a Home Rule Act, authorizing the setting up of a Dublin Parliament with limited powers, was put upon the English Statute Book.

The first effect of this new situation was shown in N.E. Ulster. Encouraged by English Unionists, the Orangemen declared their hostility to the Act, and their determination to wreck it so far as Ulster was concerned. Sir Edward Carson, the Orange leader, began at once to enrol a volunteer force and to import arms from Germany.

This was a chance not to be missed by Tom Clarke and the Brotherhood. If England would not interfere with Irishmen arming themselves to prevent the operation of a British Act of Parliament, it could not interfere with Irishmen who armed themselves ostensibly to defend it. A meeting was held in the largest hall in Dublin to enrol recruits for an Irish Volunteer Army in defence of the Home Rule Act.

But to Tom Clarke and the Irish Republican Brotherhood it was the opportunity to bring their men out into the open and to drill and arm them for the next revolt. The meeting was crowded to overflowing. Thousands of young men were eager to be enrolled, and thousands more were recruited in the country. John Redmond took alarm and did the only thing left to him. He approached the Executive of the Volunteers and asked for representation upon it for his nominees. To avoid a split, this was granted, but the aims of the two sections were diametrically opposed, and this became apparent a few months later with the outbreak of the European War.

To the IRB, the Volunteers were to make 'England's difficulty Ireland's opportunity' and to fight for Ireland against England at home. Redmond's idea was that they should be used to hold Ireland *for* England against a possible invasion of England's enemies; and when, without consulting the Executive Council, he pledged them for this purpose in the British House of Commons, and, from recruiting platforms in Ireland, appealed for recruits for the British Army in Flanders, cohesion was no longer possible. The Volunteers broke up into two sections – the Irish Volunteers controlled by the original Executive Council, and the National Volunteers controlled by John Redmond.

Meanwhile, the English Parliament passed a suspensory Act to prevent the Home Rule Act from coming into force, and at a meeting of the Supreme Council of the Irish Republican Brotherhood held in August 1914 it was decided that the war should not be allowed to end without a rising in arms. Lord Salisbury, after the Boer War, had taunted the Irish Parliamentary Party with the fact that he had been able to withdraw every British soldier fit for active service out of Ireland. The IRB decided that a similar boast should not be made in their day. They had no illusions about what the end of the revolt would be, but they believed that in suffering the extreme penalties which would follow, they would reawaken their countrymen to faith in the old cause of Irish freedom, which was being overlaid by the conciliatory policy of the Parliamentarians.

On Easter Monday, 1916, Ireland rang with the news that the Volunteers had risen in Dublin. The Rising, during which Dublin was held for a week, was made by 687 men, including the soldiers of the Irish Citizen Army under James Connolly, a Republican Socialist.

The Rising was not only a renewal of the age-long struggle for national liberation, but was a protest against the continued British occupation while England was professedly fighting a war in Europe to free small subject nationalities from the domination of the Central Powers. The advertisement given by the European War to the principle of self-determination did much to rouse and stimulate to action many in Ireland who might not otherwise have resorted to extreme measures, and determined them to draw attention to the fact that the principle was not being applied to one of the oldest nations in Europe. Among the 687 Irishmen who left their homes on that historic Easter Monday with little hope of ever returning to them, were men of education and high position whose names were known and respected by their countrymen.

The surrender was followed by the execution of sixteen leaders, including Tom Clarke, aged seventy-four, and Seán MacDermott; sentences of death, commuted to penal servitude for life or long terms of years upon seventy-one other persons, including William Cosgrave, then Minister of Local Government and President of the Executive Council of the Irish Free State since 1922, and one woman, Countess Markiewicz; and the imprisonment without trial of thousands who were suspected to have taken part or been in sympathy with the Rising, or to have been connected in any way with the Volunteers, Sinn Féin or any other patriotic organization.

While the Rising itself was unpopular, sprung as a surprise upon the country, the effect of the death sentences and imprisonments was immediate. A wave of passionate patriotism swept over the country amongst the relatives and friends of the sufferers, and all nationalist Ireland began to turn to the men, dead or imprisoned, whom they hailed as the lineal descendants of their national martyrs.

A more practical result came from the throwing together in the internment camps in England of thousands of young Irishmen. Men came together who might never have met otherwise. Hardy, stalwart Gaels from the South and the West found themselves the daily and nightly companions of the more thoughtful men of the towns and cities, who had worked out in detail their plans for the freedom and regeneration of Ireland. With their release at Christmas 1916, and during 1917, the prisoners brought home with them a new spirit of comradeship, of faith in themselves and their fellows, fresh energy, detailed plans of reorganization and supreme confidence in their power to achieve success.

They were received in Dublin, and in the towns and villages to which they returned, with scenes of wild enthusiasm and lavish welcome. The torrent of national feeling, such as had never been known before, swept away in its course the power of the Irish Parliamentary Party and the moderate counsels for which it stood.

But unlike similar situations in the past, when the patriotic fervour aroused passed away with the passing of the events which produced it, there were leaders and a policy ready by which the national emotion could be directed into channels where it could be used effectively.

Arthur Griffith was not in the Rising, but he was arrested in the general round-up which followed. On his release with the other prisoners, he was ready with his definite, constructive policy of Sinn Féin. He had been preparing for years for such a situation. He had got at last what he believed was alone wanted for the success of his policy – the support of the people.

On his release from Frongoch Internment Camp, Michael Collins, whose powers were beginning to be recognized, threw himself into the work of reorganizing the Volunteers.

By their genius, sincerity and devotion, these two men, and the other young leaders co-operating with them, seized a situation such as had never before arisen in Ireland, and used it to bring the national cause to a successful issue.

From the time of the release of the prisoners during 1916 and 1917 until the General Election at the end of the war in December 1918, Sinn Féin was busy perfecting its organization, selecting candidates, conducting by-elections and building up an election machine. The Volunteers were being drilled and new recruits enrolled for the greater struggle which was felt by all to be impending, and Michael Collins was smuggling in arms and creating and organizing a national Secret Service which was to be ready for any eventualities.

Michael Collins was the first leader Ireland ever had who recognized intelligently wherein lay England's power to render all national movements abortive, and who had the character to stand up to it and reply to it unflinchingly. That power lay in the completeness and thoroughness of the British Secret Service in Ireland.

Throughout the country the Royal Irish Constabulary (the RIC) was not a mere police force for the protection of the civil population, such as exists in other countries. The work of this police [force] was mainly political. They were armed. Their numbers were far in excess of what was required for a country notoriously free from civil crime. A village where ordinary offences against the law were practically unknown was 'guarded' by three or four policemen resident in a barracks stocked with arms and ammunition. They were all engaged in secret service activities. It was an important part of their duties to know everyone, and to know the political opinions, moderate or extreme, of everyone in their district. The RIC were 'the eyes and the ears' of the British authorities, without which they were powerless to deal with any political situation which might arise, and without whose knowledge a British Army coming into the country was helpless.

In Dublin this part of the British machine was established more openly. There were the detectives of the political branch of the Dublin Metropolitan Police, known as 'G Men'. It was these agents in the city, and those who were brought up from the country for the purpose, and the RIC in the country districts, who were used by the British military after the Rising to point out the men for court martial and subsequent execution or imprisonment, and without whom they could not have been identified. Michael Collins' intelligence department was created to counteract such activities in the future.

All was prepared, and all that was needed was a clear mandate from the people. It came with the General Election of December 1918, when Sinn Féin swept the whole of Ireland, winning seventy-three seats out of the total of 105.

Arthur Griffith, elected for Cavan, was now in a position to put his policy into execution. A National Parliament, Dáil Éireann, was set up, in which the people's representatives could assemble to carry out their election pledges. Departments of Finance, Defence, Trade and Commerce, Home Affairs, Labour, and Propaganda were established. Ministers were appointed. The Volunteers became automatically the defence force of the new government and were known henceforth as the Irish Republican Army, or the IRA.

The British Government declared Dáil Éireann an illegal assembly, and warrants were issued for the arrest of its Ministers and members, and of the leaders of the army. To effect this, the RIC in the country and the G men in the capital were brought into action. Their training was to come again into use. The Sinn Féin reply was obvious. The IRA set out to defend its parliament and to protect its members and the officers and soldiers of the army, and Michael Collins mobilized his new force to the counter-attack.

In January 1920 the Municipal Elections, and in June 1920 the Rural Elections, confirmed the Sinn Féin victory at the polls.

Dáil Éireann continued to meet – in secret. Its Ministers put forward their proposals, which were debated and voted upon. Their decisions were made public and approved by the people, who more and more obeyed their decrees, looked to them for good government and gave them their whole-hearted support. A National Loan of £400,000 was raised by Michael Collins, who had been made Minister of Finance. This sum was collected though the loan was declared illegal, though it was an illegal act to subscribe to it, to ask subscriptions for it, or to paste up a notice advertising it, and many suffered imprisonment for these or kindred offences. Several newspapers were suppressed for advertising the loan. All the complicated business in connection with the raising and the banking, secretly, of this large sum was done by a Minister who was already outlawed and who had to work and live in hiding.

The Ministers and members of Dáil Éireann had to lie concealed, and to meet and to do their administrative business in places only known among themselves. Yet the business was done; the departments were kept going; and when one man was tracked down and arrested another was ready to step into his place.

British civil law disappeared and Dáil Éireann law took its place. Sinn Féin Courts were set up in Dublin and in twenty-seven counties, with judges chosen by the districts, at which justice was administered to the satisfaction of the people. They continued in spite of the fact that when the court was discovered it was raided by the police and the officials arrested. Sinn Féin Police maintained order, and arrested criminals and restored stolen property, while themselves risking arrest and death at the hands of the British armed forces. While those forces closed fairs and markets and burned down creameries, factories and stocks of food, the Sinn Féin departments of government were busy with the development of natural resources, the revival of Irish industry and commerce, and the proper cultivation of the soil.

A commission of experts was appointed to investigate and report upon the natural resources of the country and their proper utilization, and held sittings at many places, though harassed by raids of the British forces. A National Bank was established. In the congested districts of the West, where the 'mere Irish' had been driven by Cromwell's soldiers 'to hell or Connacht', the people had struggled for centuries in a state of semi-starvation on holdings created out of the bog by their own work, surrounded by wide, untenanted grass lands. Dáil Éireann established a Land Commission and Arbitration Courts, which took steps to appease the land hunger. The courts, which Mr Lloyd George boasted he had driven into cellars, re-settled 80,000 acres and made and enforced awards which restored peace in districts which were on the verge of a serious land war.

But the British Government still affected to believe that 'it was a sham and a fraud, the whole of this nationality' and that 'a small body of assassins was dominating the country and terrorizing it'. They still 'hoped for good results from maintaining the pressure'.

Sixty thousand British troops already occupied Ireland, in addition to the armed RIC, and 15,000 'Auxiliaries' and 'Black and Tans' were drafted into it. 'It is common knowledge,' said *The Times*, 'that the Black and Tans were

recruited from ex-soldiers for a rough and dangerous task.'
At first their outrages were denied. They were then excused
as spontaneous outbreaks under intolerable provocation,
and the burning and looting in Limerick were referred to
by the General in his Farewell Order as 'an over-zealous
display of loyalty'.

More than a hundred towns were deliberately sacked.
The destruction of Balbriggan, which was near to Dublin
and famous for its hosiery works, could not be concealed,
and the *Manchester Guardian* had an article headed 'An
Irish Louvain'. *The Times*, in a leading article, said: 'The
accounts of the arson and destruction by the military at
Mallow in County Cork as revenge for a Sinn Féin raid
which caught the 17th Lancers napping on Tuesday, must
fill English readers with a sense of shame.' The Report
of the Irish Agricultural Society for the year ending 31st
March 1921, said: 'The national damage, resulting from
over fifty attacks – over sixty, indeed, if fourteen raids on
one Society are to be separately included – cannot yet be
exactly stated, but will, it is estimated, exceed £200,000.'
Town halls and private houses were soaked with petrol and
burned. Country villages were shot up, and women and
children driven in terror from their blazing homes through
streets raked with rifle volleys.

The British administration could no longer be regarded
as a government maintaining law and order, and bringing

criminals to justice, or even suppressing a political movement. It was the military organization of an enemy power waging war on the Irish nation by the methods of ruthlessness which the British had condemned elsewhere.

Between April and August 1920 coroners' juries had returned twenty-two verdicts of wilful murder or unjustifiable homicide against British military and constabulary, all of which were recorded in the Press. On 3rd September an Order-in-Council was issued making coroners' inquests illegal in ten counties. When killings took place in other counties, Dublin Castle got over the difficulty by issuing special orders that no inquests were to be held in those cases. During September and October, thirty-seven deaths by violence took place which were circumstantially charged against the armed forces of the crown. No inquest was held in any of those cases, and when any enquiry was held by the British military, it was conducted in secret. The answers given to these charges by the English Ministers were founded on the reports of the officials. The stock answers so supplied were that the shooting was done by Republicans disguised as forces of the crown, or by persons unknown, or by the forces of the crown in the execution of their duty. In no case was there any opportunity of testing the reports of the persons implicated, on which these answers were based.

Even so, the British were not 'getting the right men'.

High prices were placed on the heads of highly desired victims. Broadcast appeals were issued for anonymous accusations, with assurances that the evidence would be kept secret. The notorious convict Hardy was released and employed as an agent provocateur. It was known that a list had been prepared of persons obnoxious to the British, of whom 'a definite clearance' was contemplated.

British officers, not wearing uniforms, were lodged under false names in private apartments in Dublin. During the day they secretly collected their 'intelligence' by means of spies and touts. At night, when under the curfew regulations everyone had to be indoors, they issued forth on mysterious errands. When persons were found shot, no impartial enquiry was permitted. Soldiers of the IRA, in their duty of defending the lives of their Ministers, officers and private civilians, shot the disguised British Secret Service men and detectives of the RIC, and for doing so they were held up to the world by the British Government as 'murderers'. What is certain is that, by the efficiency of Michael Collins' leadership and the thoroughness of his intelligence service, the British were defeated on the lines on which they had always been successful hitherto. Without her spies, England was helpless. The national defence was made strong where it had hitherto been weak. The Irish by their superior intelligence and boldness outwitted the vastly superior resources of the adversary.

Dáil Éireann had not only to function, but, if it were to survive, it had to prevent the British administration from functioning. The latter's power to collect Irish money to carry out what was now purely a military régime of oppression had to be brought to an end. It was with this object in view that the burning of Income Tax records, and of the documents and records of Customs and Excise which involved the destruction of the Custom House, was decreed by Dáil Éireann, as described by the author of this story. Though the loss of men on the Irish side through the capture of so large a number of the IRA in the Custom House was severe, the loss of power and control by the British was far more serious. It brought their ability to collect money in Ireland, and to continue any kind of civil administration, practically to an end.

The Sinn Féin faith of Arthur Griffith was justified. The right and the power of the Irish people to be in control in their own country was established. The attempt of the British military organization to destroy the national Sinn Féin Government failed. The Commission appointed by the Society of Friends to visit Ireland reported: 'The British Government has ceased to function over eighty per cent of Ireland. Moderate people and many Unionists admit the only protection they enjoy is provided by the Sinn Féin police. Safety is only found in districts from which the English military and police are withdrawn. Prominent

Unionists have served on the Sinn Féin Agricultural and other Commissions.'

Ireland was not being dominated or terrorized by any small body of Irishmen, but was organizing itself with a remarkable aptitude for orderly freedom in circumstances of difficulty and danger which would have daunted a people of less high spirit, intelligence and patriotic unity. The last phase of the British violence was directed not against any 'small band of assassins', any 'real murder gang', but against the Irish people. And for this reason – that it had not been 'provoked' by any murders. The 'intolerable provocation' had been not to the outraged humanity and loyalty of the Black and Tans, but to the imperial pride of the British Government. The 'outrage' was the pushing out of the British Government and the successful establishment of a national Government in its place.

Mr Lloyd George, by an impromptu retort in the House of Commons, inadvertently let out that he was waging a war in Ireland. Mr Bonar Law blurted out the real reason for the British violence. The National Government 'had all the symbols and all the realities of government'. When that admission had been made, the end could not long be delayed.

Two hostile nations were facing one another, each with its own government and army. No peace could be found except by a public recognition of that fact and by direct negotiation between the plenipotentiaries of each side, as the authorized representatives of two equal nations. There was not room for two governments and two armies in Ireland. One or the other must go. Which had the right and the might to prevail? When the British Prime Minister proposed the unfettered conference, and a truce was agreed to on that footing, this question had already been answered and the long-drawn struggle between the nations had ended with a victory for Ireland.

Dáil Éireann at last met openly. By the authority of Ireland's elected representatives negotiations were entered into between the two belligerent nations in order to find a basis of peace. In those negotiations what had the Irish to rely on against an infinitely more powerful nation? Was it the strength which they had gathered from the justice of their cause? Was it that they had made the most of their slender military resources, not only with skill, endurance and courage, but with a humanity which could not fail to be contrasted with the British methods during the struggle?

Not only to the Irish race throughout the world, but to all persons of generous and imaginative sympathy, the story of the Irish struggle of 1918 to 1921 is an inspiring one. The people of a small and weak nation, without training, and practically without resources, by their grit, their steadfastness, their amazing solidarity (a whole people acting with one mind), and by their genius to create and build up in the midst of violence and destruction, were able to render powerless to defeat them a mighty Empire, with all the resources of wealth and power, which had been holding them in subjection for seven hundred years.

AUTHOR'S PREFACE

In April of this year, 1929, I began to write down the following pages telling of my experiences as a Volunteer and intelligence officer in the struggle (1917–1921) for independence in Ireland.

I did so at the urgent request of one or two of my friends who represented to me that those who had personal knowledge should place on record an authentic account of the doings of the Dublin Brigade of the Irish Volunteers. It was put to me further that such an account might serve to show future generations of young Irishmen how a successful fight may be made in spite of many and great disadvantages, and against what might seem to be insuperable odds.

I have mentioned no incident of which I had not personal knowledge, and although certain names and places are not particularized, I have not intentionally omitted any fact or feature of the story. I have added nothing, nor have I sought to embellish the truth anywhere. Many of my comrades are still living and are witnesses to the accuracy of my narrative.

This book being confined to my own story leaves

untouched the field of the personal experiences of my comrades, the record of which would be of the greatest interest. I believe there was not a single Volunteer who took an active part in the struggle but whose adventures were of a sensational nature.

It was from the survivors of the Dublin Brigade of the Irish Volunteers who took part in the Rising of 1916 that the later organization was built up. From that reorganized brigade came the men who made so successful a resistance to the intensive campaign of violence developed by the British under the regime of the Black and Tans.

As my story deals exclusively with the activities of men who belonged to one or other of the battalions (mainly the 2nd), it may not be out of place for me to give an idea of the formation of the Brigade:

1st Battalion. Area, North Liffey and West O'Connell Street.

2nd Battalion. Area, North Liffey and East O'Connell Street.

3rd Battalion. Area, South Liffey.

4th Battalion. Area, south townships, Rathmines, etc.

5th Battalion. Engineers only.

6th Battalion. Area, South County Dublin, Dun Laoghaire.

Each battalion was made up of six or seven companies.

The Brigade was commanded by Dick McKee. The vice-brigadier was Peadar Clancy. After the death of these two men in the Castle on the 21st November 1920, Oscar Traynor became brigadier and Patrick Mooney, vice-brigadier.

The Active Service Unit, which co-operated with the original Squad of less than a dozen Volunteers, was organized towards the end of 1920. It acted as a separate unit until the Truce in July 1921. There were about fifty Volunteers in the Active Service Unit. They were whole-time men, having left their employment to serve. Their pay in each case was at the same rate as they had been earning in civil employment.

As to the numbers fighting on each side – at the height of the struggle the figures of the British forces were given as 60,000 regular troops and 15,000 'Auxiliaries' and 'Black and Tans', in addition to the forces of the Royal Irish Constabulary. On our side the numbers are more difficult to ascertain. The nominal strength of the Dublin Brigade was 13,500, but of these not more than 1,000 were armed and not more than fifteen per cent were free to take part in action. Except the Active Service Unit, the Volunteers could only operate when they could get away from their civil jobs. Michael Collins was heard to say on more than one occasion that in the whole of Ireland there were not more than 3,000 fighting men.

Chapter I

For us in Ireland '1916' is only another name for the Rising of Easter Week. I was thirteen years old in that year, having been born in January 1903.

I was playing around my home in North Dublin on that Easter Monday, when I heard that the Volunteers had seized the General Post Office and other buildings in O'Connell Street, and that they had erected barricades across the streets leading to the positions they occupied.

The news of the Rising came as a great surprise to me, and I was most anxious to go into town and find out what was happening. When we sat down to dinner, my father told us that a party of Lancers had ridden down O'Connell Street and that they had been fired on by the Volunteers, a few of the soldiers and horses being killed.

He said there would be terrible work now, and, perhaps reading my thoughts, he told me that on no account was I to go into town. He advised my mother to lay in provisions and to buy two hundred-weight of flour.

'God knows how long this trouble will last,' he said. 'It may be a case of every ha'penny being needed to buy food.'

I had a ha'penny in my pocket, and I put my hand in and

gripped it tightly, as I was greatly affected by my father's words.

After dinner, I went out again and found my playfellows, and we decided that it would be dangerous to go into the city. We could hear the sound of the firing. So we began to play cards. The boys all condemned the Rising; they called the Volunteers 'hot-heads' and other insulting names. This made me very angry. However, at the cards – in which I had been rather unwilling to join after my father's words, fearing to lose my ha'penny – I had the satisfaction of winning and increasing my capital by two pence. It gave me even greater satisfaction that I, who was for the 'Rebels', had beaten those who were against them. I felt almost as if I were helping my heroes who were making the real fight not far away.

As the days passed, the noise of the guns grew louder and temptation got the better of me, so that I decided that I would venture to find out for myself what was happening.

I had not gone very far towards the city when I found my way barred by a cordon of military stretched across the North Circular Road. They would not allow anyone to pass except those who had entered the city to get bread at the bakery. There were no deliveries of bread made at all during that week.

I felt that I should love to join the 'Rebels', but the sound of the firing frightened me. If only I had been older

I would have helped in the fight, because maybe then, I thought, I would not have been afraid of the terrible noise made by the rifles and machine guns.

I rambled along close to the military line, not able to tear myself away. I was greatly disgusted to see women coming out of the houses to give jugs of tea to the British soldiers. That picture remained in my mind for a long time.

On the fourth or fifth morning I was talking to my mother in her bedroom. All the younger children were there too, for some reason. Suddenly the windows shook with the noise of a deafening explosion. I thought the city was being blown up and I found myself trembling. Then I heard my mother laughing. 'Look, Charlie,' she said, 'your hair is standing on end.' I was far too frightened even to smile.

What had happened? Everyone in our road ran to their hall doors to ask each other the same question, which none of them could answer. But they all expressed some opinion. One said: 'It is the artillery. The Rebels will all be killed now, and the fighting will be over. That will be a good thing, anyhow.'

Another said: 'It is the Germans landing at Howth to help the Rebels.'

The next day we learned that the explosions were caused by the gunboat *Helga*, which had been brought up the Liffey to shell the buildings occupied by the Volunteers.

That night, when we were all, as usual, gathered together upstairs to say the Rosary and to pray for the Volunteers, we did not light any lamps, thinking it too dangerous to show a light. In the dark, with the unaccustomed feeling it gave me of something solemn and mysterious, I prayed with great fervour, beseeching God to let my heroes win.

When we had finished praying I looked out of the window towards the city, where my thoughts always were, and I saw the sky all lit up with a red blaze. We thought the whole city must be on fire. This sight added to my feeling that everything was changed; that all that was safe, familiar and commonplace had disappeared.

We had to wait until the next morning to find out the meaning of it. A man who passed by our house told us that the General Post Office was in flames and that the Volunteers had surrendered. He had seen them lined up on the footpaths, he said, with a military guard around them.

I was terribly disappointed at this news. I had hoped with my whole heart that the Volunteers would win.

Chapter II

With the surrender, the newspapers began to appear again, and everyone rushed to buy them to read all about the 'Rebellion'.

A British General named Sir John Maxwell issued an official statement, telling how he had crushed the Rebels and executed their leaders.

We were horrified at this news and it created a reaction of feeling among those who had been condemning the Volunteers. Everyone now spoke in their favour. They were referred to as 'those brave men who had the courage to face untold odds for an ideal'. The 'hot-heads' were now called 'patriots' and 'idealists'. 'They were Irishmen, anyway,' they said, though some of my friends still used the word 'misguided'.

I began at once to collect souvenirs and papers dealing with the Rising. Whenever I could get a photograph of one of the dead leaders I treasured it with a kind of sacred interest.

I could now go into the city and walk among the ruins. This became my favourite occupation for a long time. I walked amongst them with a feeling of sadness, and at the same time of holiness and exultation. The streets were now so changed in appearance that to visualize what they were like before the Rising I had to look at the photographs labelled 'Before' in the souvenir albums. I made mental pictures of what the fight must have been like when it was in progress. I reconstructed the whole of the Rising, with loud rifle fire from the Post Office, and the English falling killed and wounded in the street. I searched the lanes and alleys in the area of the fighting, thinking how the Volunteers might have used them to make their escape. In Moore Lane, I looked for a long time at the spot where The O'Rahilly fell. He had been killed by British machine-gun fire while retreating from the burning General Post Office. It was in this building that the Volunteers had had their headquarters, and from which the Republican declaration was issued and Pádraig Pearse had given his order to his followers to lay down their arms.

I felt now that I would like to meet some fellow sympathizers, who would share my feelings, but I did not know where to find them. Then, one day, some weeks, or maybe a month or two after, I read in the paper that a Mass was to be offered for the dead patriots in Church Street Church at 11 o'clock on the following Sunday.

When I arrived I found the church filled with people. After Mass, I waited outside, and the congregation, mainly women, gathered round a young, red-haired man who began to sing 'Rebel' songs, in which the crowd joined whenever they knew the words. I recognized the young man as a senior schoolfellow of mine, whose sympathies I had not suspected until that moment. He was Ernie O'Malley, who afterwards played a great part in the fight in the country.

When the songs were finished, someone produced a tricolour flag. This was the signal for cheers. The crowd then formed up behind the flag-bearer and we marched in processional order through the city by College Green. That was a day of great happiness for me. I had a wonderful, proud feeling, walking in the procession. There were only a few hundred of us, and nobody seemed to mind us or take any notice of us; only a young lady who passed by linking a British officer in uniform gave us a scornful look.

These Masses were held frequently and enabled me to become one of the crowd who attended them, though I knew no one but O'Malley.

Chapter III

Besides the sixteen leaders who were executed after the Rising, thousands had been shipped to England, some to serve sentences of penal servitude, others for imprisonment in internment camps.

When it became known in December 1916 that an amnesty had been declared, there was great excitement in Dublin. The prisoners were to be released and were to be sent home at once.

Though no civic or public welcome was arranged, a great crowd of people assembled at Westland Row railway station to see the homecoming. I left home that day, not to go to school as I pretended, but to see for myself the men I so much admired and whom I hoped to join some day soon.

I waited outside Fleming's Hotel in Gardiner Place. I heard that the prisoners would come there, and others must have heard it too, because there were hundreds waiting in the road and on the pavements.

Suddenly a voice shouted: 'Here they are!'

Immediately several brakes filled with laughing, hatless men came rattling up the street. Some of them were waving their convict caps and shouting madly and singing 'The Soldier's Song', which is now our National Anthem.

They went into the hotel. We were cheering ourselves hoarse, and I never thought I could have made my voice shout so loud.

Then a tall, dark, spectacled man appeared at one of the hotel windows. When we saw him, the shouting increased. I thought he would make a speech and I was disappointed when he moved back from the window without taking any notice of our cries.

He was de Valera.

I knew that he was one of the leaders of Easter Week, and the last commandant to surrender. That was a proud moment for me when, at last, I saw face-to-face one of the heroes who filled all my dreams.

CHAPTER IV

After the prisoners had come home, having my ears always open for news, I heard that the Volunteers were reorganizing and were holding recruiting meetings.

I had a schoolmate named O'Neill, and he and I decided that we would join the Volunteers. After some trouble, we discovered that a company held their meeting each week in the Painters' Hall in Gloucester Street.

On the next meeting night we presented ourselves at the hall, and asked for the captain, a man named Colbert. We had found out his name in the course of our enquiries. We were rather troubled about our school clothes and short breeches.

'Why do you want to join the Volunteers?' he asked, looking us over in a way we did not like.

'To fight for Ireland,' we both answered.

Then he took our names and addresses and asked us our ages.

This was the question we were both dreading. I said I was eighteen and O'Neill gave his age as eighteen also. But we could not convince him that we were old enough.

'I will pass your names on to the Fianna,' (Irish Scouts) he said.

We were disgusted to hear such a proposal.

'I will not join the Fianna,' said I, 'I want to become a Volunteer.'

'My decision is final,' he replied, rather pompously, and he was just going to dismiss us when he said suddenly: 'How did you find out where to come?'

I thought this was our chance. Since we know the meeting place he will take us into his company, if only to keep us quiet, flashed through my mind.

But he thought otherwise. 'My decision is final,' he said again, as if he liked the sound of those words.

I told my troubles to a man named Hugh Casey, who had fought in the Rising. He promised to do his best for me. Casey kept his word, and though I had to face the same difficulties again, Casey's influence prevailed. I became a Volunteer. I was now fourteen years of age.

On the 25th September, just before I was enrolled, we were thrown into mourning by the tragic death of one of our leaders, Tomás Ashe. He had been arrested and sentenced to a year's imprisonment for a speech. With a number of other prisoners he had gone on hunger strike, and died from the effects of forcible feeding.

I joined the throng which filed past his bier in the Mater Hospital, whither he had been brought a few hours before his death. I was deeply moved at the sight of that splendid Irishman in his death sleep. He was dressed in his green Volunteer uniform. Passing by the bed on which he was laid out, I saw those in front of me stooping reverently to kiss his forehead. But, feeling that such a salute would be unbecoming in one who was about to become a soldier, I just placed my hand for a moment on his brow. I drew back, startled by its coldness. This was my first meeting with death. I was profoundly stirred and, at the same time, frightened.

He was buried in Glasnevin cemetery on the following Sunday. I read in the paper that he was to be given a national funeral, and of the marshalling arrangements of the Volunteers. Wishing to take part, I knew I would have no chance of being admitted to the ranks after my experience with Colbert. So, not to be defeated in my purpose, I turned up at the place allotted to 'country contingents'. I pretended to the Volunteer steward that I was a country Volunteer, a statement I counted upon him being unable to disprove.

Chapter V

It was on the 6th December 1917 that I was admitted into the Volunteers.

Casey brought me to the meeting place – a disused garage adjoining Clonliffe College, in the suburbs. The captain looked dubious when I said I was eighteen and would have sent me away, but Casey drew him on one side and spoke to him in a whisper.

The captain told me to go to a little room at the end of the garage, where I would find the quartermaster. The QM was a Corporation official. His tousled hair and harassed expression, as he scanned the papers scattered all over the table at which he was sitting, gave the impression that he could not quite cope with all he had to do. After taking down particulars he gave me a membership card and asked for my subscription.

When he mentioned 'subscription', I nearly died. But when he said 'threepence' my relief was immense, as I had exactly three coppers in my pocket. It was only good luck that I had any money at all.

He informed me that by paying into the Arms Fund I would get a revolver as soon as any were available. This pleased me immensely, as I felt that once I was armed I would be a real soldier.

My new comrades held a weekly meeting or parade. The company was divided into four sections of about twenty-five men each, grouped according to the localities in which they lived. I was allotted to No. 4 Section.

The men were mainly labourers and unskilled workers, but within the ranks were men of widely different callings and ages. I learned that, with a few exceptions, the men had no arms. But the company possessed a .22 miniature rifle, a weapon on which scores of us afterwards learned the rudiments of musketry.

The first night I paraded, an election of officers was held, as the captain had been promoted to the battalion staff. I did not know the men who were elected, but I was told that they had all fought in the Rising, as indeed had many of the men with whom I was on parade.

I noticed that prompt obedience was made to the orders given from the lance corporal upwards. Everyone seemed anxious to show his willingness.

Though carried out as quietly and secretly as possible, our activities soon came under the notice of the police, which produced the first signs of official activity since the Rising was suppressed.

Chapter VI

When I was on my way home from school one day in April 1918, I met a Volunteer belonging to my company. He told me that he had been mobilized to go to the Corporation Yard of the Cleansing Department in Portland Place.

'There is a job on there,' he said, 'and any NCOs or idle men of the Battalion are required.'

I was overjoyed to hear this good news. A job was on. Here was a chance at last for me to do something.

I turned back and went straight to the yard. Some people and a few policemen were gathered outside. I knocked at the big gates. They were opened only a crack and I was asked what I wanted. I gave the letter of my company and the number of my battalion. At once, as if by magic, the gate was thrown wide open for me to enter. I walked in holding my head very high, feeling the eyes of the people outside watching me with curiosity and envy. *Who is that boy who is so privileged?*, I fancied they were saying to themselves. *He must be somebody of importance.*

Inside, there were twenty or thirty Volunteers at work. The yard was strewn with the carcasses of pigs, which had been slaughtered by one of the Volunteers who was a butcher by trade. Two droves of pigs had been seized earlier in the day on their way from the market to the quay. This had been done by order of the Sinn Féin Food Controller, Diarmuid Lynch, to stop the wholesale exportation of pigs while the curing factories at home were practically idle.

Some of the Volunteers were occupied in cleaning the carcasses, and I was given a yard brush and was told to sweep up the blood which was being hosed into the channel. I felt very superior engaged in this work of national importance.

While I was busy in this way, for some reason the gates were opened and the crowd outside could now see what was going on.

'Ah, isn't it a terrible shame,' they exclaimed, 'to be wasting all that blood which would make such grand black puddings' (a breakfast sausage which is highly valued in Ireland). That was the first time I heard of the origin of that delicacy.

When our work was done, which had taken some hours, and the yard was cleaned up, the carcasses were loaded on lorries. By now a great crowd had gathered outside, and women handed us in jugs of tea and slices of bread.

I drank the tea with great satisfaction, recalling the time when I had seen the very same refreshments handed to the British Tommies in my neighbourhood during the Rising. The tide had turned. It was we who were now the heroes of the people.

It was nightfall when we emerged into the street with our cargo. We formed up in processional order with a file of Volunteers on each side of the 'hearses'. We marched in mournful triumph across the city to the curing factory where the bodies were handed over.

I had wondered why the large force of police, which had waited outside the yard all the afternoon, had made no attempt to interfere with us. In fact, I was disappointed, as we had all armed ourselves with heavy sticks. I heard afterwards that the owners of the droves refused to make a charge as they had been paid the value of the pigs by the Food Controller.

Dramatic accounts of this incident appeared in the newspapers. It gave me a feeling of elation to receive this public recognition of what was my first job.

Chapter VII

On a beautiful morning in 1918 we were mobilized to meet at Artane, a village a couple of miles outside Dublin.

When I got to the rendezvous I was surprised to find a great crowd of men waiting about in small groups. Many of them I had never seen before and I knew that they did not belong to my company. It was only when a whistle was blown and I heard the 'Fall in' order shouted that I realized that the whole battalion, some five hundred men, were on parade.

At the words of command we marched off in column of route. Everyone seemed very happy at this display of defiance of the official proclamations forbidding illegal assemblies and drilling.

After marching for about two miles through country lanes, we turned into a big field and our first manoeuvres began. While I was occupied in taking part in them, which I did with great pride and earnestness, I noticed a man with a bicycle talking privately to our brigadier, Dick McKee. I had seen this man earlier in the day posted on the road we had traversed to warn us of the approach of the police.

I thought his appearance must be the forerunner of

ill news, and, sure enough, shortly afterwards two RIC entered the field. They watched us with apparent interest, but made no attempt to interfere with us, which, indeed, would have been difficult considering our numbers, and we continued drilling, taking no notice of their presence.

After three or four hours of military exercises, we returned to the road and began our march home. We had not proceeded very far when I caught sight of clouds of dust ahead of us and two large military lorries came into view. When they reached the head of our column they were pulled up and about thirty armed policemen jumped out, barring our way.

Excitement and confusion followed. They were arresting our officers, including the brigadier. They were put in a lorry. One Volunteer, bolder than the rest of us, picked up a stone and threw it at the police. He was immediately seized and put under arrest. The scene then took on an angry appearance and it looked as if there was about to be a fight when the brigadier addressed us from the lorry, bidding us to hold our peace and obey his order to disperse quietly.

This was my first contact with the enemy.

Those arrested were tried and sentenced to six months' imprisonment for illegal drilling, on the evidence of the two RIC constables.

CHAPTER VIII

I was promoted to the rank of sergeant of No. 4 Section of the company, while I was still attending school.

Often on my way to school I would meet some Volunteers whom I drilled on the weekly parade night. These meetings caused me great embarrassment and, in order to make myself look older and more important, I decided that I must alter my dress. To do so, I commandeered an old pair of my father's trousers and a cap. Now I felt I looked a man and I no longer feared to meet my comrades.

At this time my brother, who was serving in France in the commissioned ranks of the British Army, returned home on leave. He brought home with him a German pistol and a rifle as souvenirs. I took possession of the pistol and was overjoyed at my acquisition, which I proudly reported to the quartermaster.

'Of course you will hand it up,' he said. 'We are very short of guns in the company.'

This I refused to do.

'If the company wants my gun,' said I, 'they can take me with it.'

If my gun was going to see service, I was determined

that I was going to be the man to use it.

Being now one of the few Volunteers who were armed, I was ordered one day by my captain to report to the Battalion QM at 46 Parnell Square for duty. I guessed that there was something on foot and I went to the appointed place full of eager expectation.

I found a score of Volunteers waiting in a large room ordinarily used as a classroom by the Gaelic League. I knew a few of them – Brigadier McKee and Peadar Clancy. In the room were also Jim Slattery, Vincent Byrne and Tom Kehoe, who were to be afterwards my comrades in many a hazardous enterprise. They were subsequently in Michael Collins' famous Squad and will come frequently into my story. I did not have any conversation with them on this occasion.

Dick McKee was a tall man, over six foot high, of soldierly bearing and fine countenance. He wore a small black moustache which added to his military appearance. He spoke with a soft drawl. And it was that beguiling voice of his, so attractive – like the tune of the Pied Piper – which cast a spell over you, so that you could not but obey him.

He was a printer in the firm of Messrs Gill and Son of O'Connell Street. He knew personally nearly every Volunteer in the brigade, and he never passed by a man he knew without giving him a glance and a smile of recognition.

Peadar Clancy was an outfitter, in partnership with

another Volunteer officer, Tom Hunter. Their shop in Talbot Street was known as 'The Republican Outfitters'. Peadar was a County Clare man. He was young and handsome, with a clear complexion and a beautiful speaking voice. He had a very gentle, engaging manner.

Dick McKee told us that we were about to undertake an important, daylight 'hold-up'.

'Robert Barton is being tried today at the Police Courts for a speech he delivered in Wicklow. He is to be rescued by us,' he said. 'He will be brought from the Courts to Mountjoy Jail in a motor van. That van must be held up.'

He then outlined the plan of action and allotted us our different positions.

While waiting for the appointed hour, a lively discussion arose as to the merits of my Mauser pistol. It was quite a new gun to most of the men present. It was generally condemned because some of our men had been badly let down by the jamming of their automatic pistols, and they had found from experience that the revolver bullet had greater stopping power.

Peadar Clancy said to me: 'The next time you are brought on a job, come with a decent weapon. If you have not got a revolver, get a loan of one somewhere.'

This made me feel extremely indignant, as I dearly loved my Mauser, so that when Dick McKee, who was listening, took my part, I was delighted.

'There is nothing wrong with that gun. I like automatics,' he said, producing a long Parabellum of his own.

Whether this was the beginning of our subsequent friendship I cannot say, but after that incident the brigadier was very friendly towards me. And as for me, I looked up to him and worshipped him.

Shortly after noon we went in groups of twos and threes to the scene of action – the corner of Mountjoy, Blessington and Nelson streets. We took up our positions without attracting the attention of the passers-by.

After waiting about fifteen minutes we saw a Ford covered-in military van approaching. As soon as it reached the corner, some of our men, who were waiting up a side street, pushed a builders' handcart, on which were some very long ladders, across the roadway, blocking the van's progress. This was the signal for us all to rush forward, pointing our guns at the occupants, and shouting 'Hands up.'

Immediately, with their hands up, an officer, Major Carew, and two Tommies stepped out of the car.

There was no one else! There was no prisoner! The authorities, anticipating the possibility of a rescue, had had Barton conveyed back to Mountjoy by another route.

During the excitement, a Volunteer accidentally discharged his revolver, wounding himself in the leg.

Major Carew, greatly agitated, shouted: 'For God's

sake, men, don't shoot,' when, seeing it was an accident, he quickly regained his composure.

Meanwhile the traffic had come to a standstill. Crowds began to collect. It was time to get away.

CHAPTER IX

It was now 1919, and I was sixteen years old.

One day I noticed a Volunteer cycling along in the neighbourhood in which I lived. I knew his business did not take him to my district, so I became suspicious that something was on foot.

Shortly afterwards I met a newsboy shouting 'Stop Press' and as I was curious I made no delay in getting a paper.

The news was startling. Lord French, the Lord Lieutenant, had been attacked at Ashtown. He and his escort were travelling in two touring cars and a van, when bombs had been thrown at them, and in the fight which followed one of the attackers was killed.

Lord French had escaped injury.

I guessed that the Volunteer I had seen had had something to do with the attack. Here was dangerous work being carried out by a select few and I was not one of them! I was disturbed by this discovery, and set myself to think how I could best avail myself of the knowledge I had gained to secure a place amongst those who were engaged on special work. To ask my captain would only make him suspicious, and he probably knew nothing of the identity of those special men.

I thought it best to await an opportunity to tackle the Volunteer I had seen. This occurred soon afterwards, and I told him what I had noticed of his movements and that I suspected him of having had a hand in the attack on Lord French.

He immediately became very reserved and tried to put me off, but I persisted. I convinced him that my only object in speaking to him was to offer my help. I wanted him to speak to his leader for me, so that I could be taken on for dangerous work. He made no promises, but he must have reported our conversation, because shortly afterwards I was picked to take part in some fairly important undertakings.

One evening I was notified that I was to call at the house of the quartermaster of the battalion on the following morning at 7 o'clock.

Mick MacDonald was a man of nearly forty years, much older than any of the other men who formed the Squad. He had very prominent temples and spoke with a shrill voice like a woman's. He was a stickler for detail and he would pour forth his wrath on anyone who was a few minutes late. That was quite right of course in a soldier, but in our war our difficulties were immense. We had always to be dodging the enemy and could not go by direct routes to keep our engagements, and at the same time, a minute one way or the other might affect the success of an enterprise.

Mick Mac took his duties with intense seriousness, and this, with his irascible temper, made it a bad business to vex him. He was very brave. His whole heart was in the fight, and knowing the shortness of our ammunition, if he had had his way, I believe he would not have given out a single cartridge without a guarantee that it would be used with effect. He could not bear six shots to be fired, when five might have done as well.

'How many did you use?' he would ask anxiously. And when he was told: 'God blast you, could you not have managed with less?'

Needless to say I was not a minute late for my appointment the following morning and I was very favourably received.

There were several men present, and now for the first time I met, to speak to, the famous Squad who worked under Dick McKee and Michael Collins, and whose achievements never failed to produce 'Stop Press' editions.

They were having breakfast, with home-made bread, and they asked me to join them, which I did with the greatest pleasure. I could hardly believe it possible that I was sitting at the same table with such fearless men, whom I had for so long admired, though till now I had never met them, or known them by name. Soon I began to feel quite at home with them, especially as they did not seem to notice that I was rather young, but treated me as one of themselves.

Tom Kehoe was one of them. He was a tall, country boy, and had no regard at all for personal danger. At the age of about seventeen he had taken part in the Rising of 1916. He was a fitter by trade, and he had started making grenades in a small secret bomb factory we had in Parnell Street, which was seized by the Black and Tans. He was a splendid soldier and a true and loyal friend, so that we have never got over his tragic end. Having survived all the dangers of the Black and Tan period, he was killed in the Civil War.

The other two men present that morning were Jim Slattery and Vinny Byrne. Jim was from Bodyke, County Clare. Vinny was born and bred in Dublin. They were both cabinet-makers, and had served their apprenticeship together. As lads of seventeen they had fought in the Rising with Tom Kehoe, who was about the same age. Jim wore a loose-fitting dust-coat, and, in spite of his long residence in Dublin, he spoke with a pronounced, soft, Clare accent. He had very clear, penetrating, blue eyes.

Vinny was an optimist. He was pleased with all the world and everybody in it. On his round and slightly sleepy face was an expression of incurable good nature. He was a typical Dublin man.

When we had finished breakfast we came to business.

The leader outlined the plan. We were to go to the corner of Dominick Street and be in position by 8.30. When he gave the signal, we were to seize a mail van which would then be approaching us, and stand by while the mails were transferred to a waiting motor-car in an adjoining lane.

While waiting at the street corner I felt very excited, so that I could hardly control myself. But I did my best to keep as calm as possible outwardly, for fear that any signs of my excitement would result in my being dropped from further work.

Several mail vans passed by from the Rink close by, which was now being used as the Chief Sorting Office.

At last a van came which I knew was the one we wanted. Our leader gave the signal. The men, and I with them, rushed out and seized the horse's head and reins. We covered the driver with our revolvers, Tom Kehoe jumped up, and, taking the reins out of the driver's hands, he drove the van round the corner to where the motor-car was waiting.

Everything happened so quickly that the few pedestrians remained motionless, glued to the ground, as if they had suddenly become benumbed. We chased after the van and saw the safe transfer of the mails to our car. The driver was a Volunteer named Owen Cullen, who belonged to my company. He was the first driver attached to the Squad and the first whole-time Volunteer in Dublin, as he lost his job when his employers discovered that he had been engaged in Volunteer activities.

The whole affair was over in three minutes and we were on our way back to safety.

Later in the day, as soon as it appeared, I got the inevitable 'Stop Press'.

'Sensational Coup.

Robbery of Castle Mails.'

There followed detailed descriptions by 'eye-witnesses', which greatly surprised me as they were quite erroneous.

In the trams there was no other conversation. I could hear scraps of the news exchanged. 'French's mail seized!' 'A wonderful coup!' 'Such remarkable intelligence work!' 'So-and-so who knows so-and-so told me how it was done,' and here would follow an imaginary story, so that I had trouble not to interrupt and tell them what lies they were talking.

But we had to keep our mouths sealed. Not a word could we drop even to our dearest friends. Silence and success went hand in hand.

CHAPTER X

Some weeks later, a messenger called to my house and handed me a note. It was an instruction from the brigadier to report to him the following morning at a house he used as an office in Parnell Square.

To receive a command from Dick McKee himself filled me with the proudest satisfaction. I was overjoyed. I began at once to make considerable preparations for so important an interview. Not possessing a man's suit, I borrowed one of my elder brother's, so that my appearance would be worthy of the occasion. Although a little large for me I was satisfied with the result.

When I arrived at headquarters, there was a meeting of officers in progress, so that I had to wait some time before I was called in to the room.

The brigadier took me on one side and questioned me as to whether I had ever been to London.

I told him I had not, but that I was quite prepared to go there or anywhere else. I did not tell him that I had never been farther than a few miles from Dublin.

He asked me if I would be prepared to travel for a week or so, and I replied that I was at his service.

He kept looking me over, and seemed doubtful as to whether he would send me away, and, at last, as if he were summing up the matter, he said, 'I think you have horse sense, any way.'

I was greatly troubled by this description of myself, as I did not know what horse sense meant. But it must not have been detrimental, because he told me to hold myself in readiness to travel to London.

'You will be accompanied by a few men from Dublin and Cork, and you will get full instructions later.'

With these words he closed the interview.

I was greatly pleased with these prospects, and I was looking forward to seeing London and carrying out whatever work was to be done there.

But I was doomed to disappointment. Day after day passed and I received no summons. Then I heard that the job was off.

Long afterwards I learned that what we were to do in London was to watch the movements of Cabinet Ministers. But the idea was not developed owing to unfavourable reports from our intelligence officer there.

Chapter XI

For some months we had been engaged on attempted seizures of arms, some of which had been successful. The difficulty of importing arms was very great, as the ports were all closely watched. In spite of this, Michael Collins was able to get them in through secret channels, but we never had sufficient for our defence. So we supplemented our limited supplies by depriving the enemy of his arms and ammunition as often as we could.

One way of doing this was to attack the police barracks and force the occupants to surrender. As the police in Ireland were armed, the barracks were all well stocked.

During Easter 1920 I was sent for by the adjutant-general, Gearóid O'Sullivan, and was given verbal instructions which I was to take down to the OC of the Carlow Brigade. I was given a covering address, by means of which I would be able to get into touch with him.

I arrived very early at Kingsbridge Station, to make sure that I would be in time. Having questioned a porter, I made out which was the train for Carlow and I took my seat in a third-class compartment.

I had bought a newspaper, but I did not get a chance

to read it, because I was quite preoccupied with the scenery, which was new to me, and with the conversation of my fellow passengers. There were five or six of these, apparently businessmen. I decided they were commercial travellers, and they spoke in loud tones, expressing very decided political opinions. They had looked me over at the beginning of the journey and had evidently decided that I was of no importance.

The journey to Carlow, though only about fifty miles, seemed very long to me as it was the longest journey I had ever made. When we arrived at Carlow station there were two RIC men on the platform. They closely scrutinized everyone who alighted from the train, but my youthful appearance did not rouse their suspicions.

I went to the covering address and was kept waiting for some hours before I met the OC, who, I was told, was 'on the run', the police having raided his home several times looking to arrest him. I was taken to him at last to the Community House of the Christian Brothers' School.

He was a young man of about twenty-two years, tall and thin – a scholarly-looking fellow, I thought. But, maybe that was only because he was wearing glasses. He was the son of a hardware merchant in the town.

I knew him as Seán. I made myself known to him and conveyed my instructions, which I had committed to memory.

'You will burn all vacated RIC barracks on Easter Saturday night.

'You will simultaneously raid the houses of Income Tax collectors and seize all papers, which you will destroy.

'You will cause these orders to be transmitted verbally.

'Similar operations will be carried out in all areas on Saturday night.'

The English had already begun to vacate all the RIC barracks in isolated places which they could not hold. We destroyed these to prevent their subsequent re-occupation. The destruction of all Income Tax papers was ordered to prevent the British authorities from continuing the collection of Income Tax, which now properly belonged to the treasury of Dáil Éireann.

My interview with Seán over, I found I had some time to wait before the return train left for Dublin. I spent it in taking a look at the town, paying particular attention to the local barracks and the jail.

The next day I reported to the adjutant-general. He was lunching with some other staff officers in a restaurant in Henry Street. These men were all wanted by the authorities and had to move about cautiously, but the restaurant was owned by a supporter of ours and it was a fairly safe meeting-place.

He thanked me when I had made my report, and asked me to give him an account of my expenses and any change

I had over from the money he had given me for my journey. This it was easy for me to do, as I had had no expenses other than my railway fare, the people I had met in Carlow having entertained me to both dinner and tea.

That evening I received a note from my company captain telling me to call to see him.

He instructed me to pick six or seven men and gave me the address of an Income Tax collector's office in Abbey Street. This we were to raid and burn on Easter Saturday night at 7 p.m.

The office was situated opposite the Abbey Theatre, and when we arrived queues of people were lined up, waiting for the doors to be opened.

We knocked at the door of the office, but got no answer. There was no caretaker in the place, a difficulty for which we had made allowance. Not to attract attention, we separated a little and stood away from the place. One man then went to the door and quietly and unostentatiously forced it open with a short lever he had brought for the purpose.

The door offered little resistance and we all quietly entered the house. We soon located the office we wanted and proceeded to set the papers on fire. But the progress of the fire was so slow (and it was not safe for us to stay very long), that one of us, Jimmy Conroy, went round to a nearby shop and bought a bottle of paraffin oil.

After that we had no difficulty, and the office was well

on fire before we left. The papers were all burned before the Fire Brigade arrived and extinguished it. The Central Fire Office was round the corner, so they had only a few yards to come to put out the flames.

All the way home Conroy kept lamenting that the only money he had for cigarettes he had spent on paraffin.

CHAPTER XII

By this time, 1920, the fight had got very hot in Dublin. The lives of our leading men were in danger, day and night. They were being continually hunted, to be shot out of hand, if not reserved for hanging, and several G men (detectives of the political branch) had been shot to anticipate their activities in this respect. At the same time, Terence MacSwiney, the Lord Mayor of Cork, was dying on hunger strike in prison in London.

The Squad, which was now reinforced by some auxiliary workers, of which I was one, received instructions to meet one Sunday morning at 7.30.

When I arrived, I found that there were about fifteen Volunteers gathered in the vicinity of Grattan Bridge, which is the nearest bridge crossing the Liffey from Dublin Castle. There were very few people about at this hour, save those passing to and from the early Masses at a nearby church – the Church of SS Michael and John.

We stood about in groups of twos and threes, not to attract the attention of any policeman who might come along. Mick Mac came up to me and the man who was with me, and allotted us a position which we were to occupy in a maze of alleyways which approached the church. We moved into position.

A party of six or seven G men, who rarely left the Castle, were coming out just before eight. At a certain signal we were to open the attack, but without the given sign they were to be allowed to pass and nothing must be done to arouse their suspicions. A motor-car was waiting on the quay outside a hotel. A Volunteer was at the wheel, and in the event of any casualties we were to rush our wounded to the car.

We had not waited many minutes when the chapel bell rang out for Mass.

We knew that it was now five minutes to eight and that the time for action was swiftly approaching. I noticed a look of nervous tension appear on the faces of our men, and I steeled myself for what was to come.

At such moments one notices everything – something happens in oneself which corresponds to the sudden silence in a room when one becomes aware of the ticking of the clock. As the minutes passed, I found it hard to check the restless feeling that came over me. At the same time I felt that the whole world, outside the scene in which our drama was being enacted, had come to a standstill.

Then one of our men came running down the alley. He was Tom Cullen, a tall, well-built man, wearing a white sweater. He looked like an athlete, out for some early morning training. He spoke hurriedly to our leader, and whatever he said caused us to scatter.

The job was off.

Neither my companion nor I had time to move away before the party of detectives came into view. We started to walk towards them, not to arouse their suspicions, and we passed them unchallenged.

We were greatly disappointed at the failure to carry out our operation and tried to learn the reasons for it. It appeared that one of the detectives was a friend who was useful to us, and it was his presence with the others which necessitated the calling off of the attack.

However, we were to get another opportunity on the following Sunday.

Again we took up our positions as before, and again we got word that we were to disperse. I was surprised, and I greatly wondered why the job was again called off. On my way home one of my comrades told me that it had been postponed by an order from headquarters. Terence MacSwiney was reported to be near death in Brixton Jail, and it was decided that the attack would be more effective as a reprisal.

On the following Saturday, the 30th September 1920, some of us decided to go to a céilidh (a party with Irish dances), which was being held at Banba Hall. We agreed to pass the night there, so that we could be in position early on Sunday morning.

Curfew ended at 6 a.m. At that hour I left the hall in the company of Joe Leonard, a fellow Volunteer. We had promised to call for Paddy, one of our men who was living alone, and who, having no one to wake him, was afraid of sleeping too late.

The three of us, having had some tea, set out for the city, it being now 7 o'clock.

As we walked along we met only a few stragglers hurrying to Mass. Dawn was just breaking, and in the twilight we noticed a large military lorry approaching us. It drew abreast of us and we saw about a dozen Tommies, wearing tin hats, standing in the lorry.

The car was slowing down as it passed us and it came to a standstill on the canal bridge some twenty yards away. The soldiers jumped out and took up positions on the bridge.

We got ready for action in case of necessity and turned down a road at right angles to the bridge (Ossory Road), expecting every minute to hear a command to halt. With our hands on our hidden weapons we were ready to draw them, but fortunately for us we were not challenged. It was now almost certain death to be found with a gun, and there could have been only one end for us anyway.

Having walked about a hundred yards and got out of sight of the soldiers, we crossed a wall and got down on to some railway lines. Here we held a council of war to decide on our action.

Taking Paddy's gun from him, we sent him along unarmed to pass through the military and warn the other Volunteers waiting near the church of the military picket. Some of them, we knew, would return that way and, if not apprised, would fall on disaster.

From our hidden look-out we saw Paddy being searched on the bridge, and saw him being allowed to continue on his way.

The light now increased and we noticed another party of soldiers coming towards the spot where we were hiding. It was time to be on the move.

We started walking along the railway lines in full view of the soldiers. But the distance between us was too great for a voice to carry. If they challenged us we did not hear them and proceeded on our way.

The railway lines on which we were walking were elevated, and ran parallel with the Royal Canal at a distance of about 200 yards. The railway crossed the intersecting roadways by overhead bridges, and from each bridge as we crossed it we saw military standing about on the corresponding canal bridge.

We rightly concluded that the north side of the city was cut off by the military cordon occupying all the canal bridges. This meant that it was now impossible for us to join our comrades, who were waiting for the G men near the church.

We reached Drumcondra Bridge, having travelled about a mile and a half along the railway embankment. We stood watching the soldiers searching pedestrians on the canal bridge opposite us.

Just then a bell rang in a nearby convent and I knew that it was half-past eight.

The sound of the bell brought to me a vivid sense of the reality of the situation.

'Joe,' I said, 'what will we do now? The job must be over and the fellows on their way back. Will they blame us for not turning up? They will surely walk into the military.'

'Can't we do something ourselves?' he replied. 'Can't we do something to make them disperse?'

'I think we can,' I said, turning my eye towards the soldiers on the opposite bridge. Joe's eyes followed mine. We read each other's thoughts.

We knelt down on the parapet and, with my Mauser in my hand, we levelled our pistols at three of four soldiers who were standing on the footpath of the bridge. Some civilians were crossing at the time.

As soon as they had passed, I said: 'Now!'

We both pressed the triggers of our pistols and continued to do so until the magazines were empty.

Then, without waiting to see what was the effect of our fire, we ran along the railway for some hundreds of yards, until we found a spot where we could get down onto a road.

My heart was thumping with excitement and from running at such speed. Every moment I expected to hear the sound of a military lorry dashing after us.

But when we reached the road there was nobody in sight. We exchanged a look of infinite relief. Walking on to a house of a Volunteer in the neighbourhood, we gave him our guns to hide for us.

We were now close to the street in which I lived, and Joe and I called at my home, where we had breakfast, of which we were badly in need.

When we had finished, we went out again and were just in time to see the troops driving away.

We called at Mick Mac's house, and told him why we were unable to join him and that we had taken action on our own account. He asked us for the details of what had happened, but he did not seem to attach much importance to our exploit.

That night I was going home just before curfew, which was then at midnight, when a large touring car passed me. I noticed that there were several men in it, dressed as civilians. I was amazed to see the car draw up outside my house.

Immediately I scented danger. Already a number of Volunteers had been shot in midnight raids by military officers in mufti under the leadership of a Captain X.

I at once retraced my steps and made for the home of a Volunteer who lived nearby, where I spent the night.

CHAPTER XIII

I did not go home the following night, and my judgment proved very advisable.

Having failed to get me the night before, the enemy decided to raid for me officially. Troops arrived late in the evening, entered and searched the house, and finding me absent they arrested my brother, Emmet. Apparently a neighbour had seen me leaving the railway track on the morning of the scrap and had informed the authorities.

As my brother had fought in Flanders, it was not easy to keep him as a hostage for me. After a few hours' detention he was released and came home full of his experience.

I now knew that it would not be safe for me to go home again, and from this time onwards I was 'on the run'.

Brigadier McKee sent for me and questioned me very closely as to what was in my mind in firing on the British soldiers. I was dreading this interview as I expected to be court-martialled for acting without orders.

So I kept lying to him, saying that the troops had seen us and that we feared pursuit and capture. But it was plain that he was not convinced and that he believed we had acted with deliberation and without provocation, which was the truth.

Though he could not get me to admit the facts, he seemed very pleased with the affair. It appeared that two soldiers were killed by our fire, and their officers, supposing that they were being ambushed by a large party of our men, caused the cordon immediately to be withdrawn.

In the next issue of our Volunteer Weekly Paper, *An t-Óglach* (The Volunteer), which was printed and circulated secretly, I was amazed to find a paragraph quoting the incident as 'a splendid example of initiative'.

This was the first occasion on which troops had been deliberately fired on since the Rising, though in some previous attempts to disarm them some soldiers had been killed. Hitherto we had directed our action solely against their spies, either of the RIC or the intelligence department.

But now it was realized that to allow the troops to believe that they were immune from the danger of attack was tying our hands. They were raiding and searching and were operating with those who were directly employed to put an end to the National Movement and the men taking part in it.

CHAPTER XIV

A few days later one of the Squad called on me and asked me to accompany him. 'The assistant director of intelligence wants to interview you,' he told me.

He brought me into the city and through a number of side streets to Crow Street, an alleyway off Dame Street, quite close to Dublin Castle – the stronghold of the enemy.

When we came to a small printer's shop he beckoned me up the stairs, and on the second floor he knocked on the door. On the door a card was fixed, with the words in printed letters 'Irish Products Coy'.

After a little delay, a door was opened and we were admitted. There were three or four other Volunteers inside, some of whom I knew slightly. I noticed there were stacks of newspapers lying around.

Sitting at the table was a tall young man, with dark hair brushed back very smoothly. He had the look of a dominant personality. I recognized him as a Volunteer whom I had seen occasionally when there was something very important on hand.

He was Liam Tobin, the assistant director of intelligence, working immediately under Michael Collins. As a lad of nineteen he had fought in the Rising under Tom Clarke and was sentenced to death, the sentence being commuted to penal servitude for life.

After we had exchanged a few commonplace remarks, he asked me if I would like to become a member of his staff. There was nothing on earth I wished for more, but I had looked upon it as an honour far above my reach, and I was hard put to it to hide from him my eagerness and the feeling of surprise which almost overwhelmed me.

So I replied, as composedly as I could, that nothing would please me better.

He seemed satisfied with me, and forthwith instructed me in my new duties. I was to report to him the next morning and he would tell me what I was to do.

When I arrived, very punctually, the following morning, I was given the daily papers to look through. I was told to cut out any paragraphs referring to the personnel of the Royal Irish Constabulary or military, such as transfers, their movements socially, attendance at wedding receptions, garden parties, etc. These I pasted on a card which were sent to the director of intelligence for his perusal and instructions. Photographs and other data which were or might be of interest were cut out and put away. We often gathered useful information of the movements of important enemy personages in this manner, whom we traced also by a study of *Who's Who*, from which we learned the names of their connections and clubs. By intercepting their correspondence we were able to get a clue to their movements outside their strongholds.

I was next shown how to decode telegrams. Liam Tobin received copies of telegrams from some person he had working for him in the Central Telegraph Office. These were all in code and were addressed to district inspectors of the RIC throughout the country. We possessed the key word, so we had no difficulty in deciphering them. The key word was changed at least once a month, but in notifying the change the new key word was telegraphed in the existing code. So that having once got the key word the code was always afterwards decipherable by us.

The contexts of these messages usually referred to contemplated arrests and raids on Volunteers' houses. By communicating copies of these messages to the areas concerned, the police were frustrated. When the raiders arrived the men they were looking for were not at home.

Other important information was gained in this manner, without which we would have been beaten very early in the fight. The odds were so powerfully against us that we had all the time to make up by our alertness and forethought for our material deficiencies.

We compiled a list of friendly persons in the public services, railways, mailboats and hotels. I was sent constantly to interview stewards, reporters, waiters and hotel porters to verify our reports of the movement of enemy agents.

After a time I became curious to know who was the occupant of the other office on our landing, as I could hear coming from it the constant sound of a typewriter. I was told that she was a Protestant and hostile lady who was 'a typist. 'But do not be uneasy about her,' they said, 'she is quite deaf.'

Though I knew that Michael Collins was the director of intelligence, I did not see him, nor did he ever call at our office. His messenger, Joe O'Reilly, a Volunteer, came twice a day, taking letters for the D/I, and leaving letters from him for Liam Tobin. Joe came always on a bicycle and was the only medium of direct communication between the assistant director and the director of intelligence. At least, in the daytime.

I had not been engaged for more than a week on my new duties when the assistant D/I told us that he was increasing our staff. There were now about twelve men comprising the intelligence branch.

CHAPTER XV

Since the General Post Office was destroyed in the Rising of 1916, the sorting of letters had been carried on at the Rink in Parnell Square.

There had been seizures of the mails from time to time by the Volunteers, and the authorities took steps to ensure the safety of their official correspondence. Important letters were taken to the Rink for sorting and military escorts accompanied the vans carrying official letters to and from the sorting office.

A military guard had been placed over the Rink, but was withdrawn subsequently, and a system of alarms installed in its place. These consisted of several electric buttons which communicated with the Castle. Immediately one of them was pressed the alarm would ring out there, and military and armoured cars could be rushed to the Rink.

Since the withdrawal of the military guard, Michael Collins and his intelligence officers had been considering the possibility of effecting another coup.

The director of intelligence got into touch with a friendly postal official and got him to make a plan of the Rink, showing the positions of the alarm bells and also of the racks which contained the various government mails.

It was discovered that the mails were all sorted by eight o'clock in the morning and were collected by the military at nine. It was, therefore, possible that if the Rink could be entered shortly after eight o'clock and the officials taken by surprise so that they could not give the alarm, it would be a comparatively easy matter to seize the mails.

I was sent for one evening by the vice-commandant, Oscar Traynor. He showed me a very good plan of the Rink and told me that he had instructions to carry out a raid there the next morning at eight-thirty. He had picked a dozen men for the job, and I was delighted to find that I was to be one of them.

He then outlined the plan. We were to enter the rear or west side of the Rink. There were platforms there onto which the bags were unloaded from the vans, and from these platforms two chutes descended into the building down which the mail bags were discharged.

He told me that three of our intelligence officers would unobtrusively enter the front or main entrance a few minutes before our party, and would take up positions by the three alarm bells and prevent them from being sounded.

I arrived at the rendezvous, a corner a hundred yards away from the Rink, precisely at 8.25.

There I saw the other men waiting. The vice-commandant spoke to me and, taking out his watch, he waited until it wanted half a minute to half-past eight.

Then he told another man and myself to go ahead, and to bear in mind the position of the chutes. The rest of the men would follow us at a little distance behind, as if the postmen, who were on the platform unloading the mails, were to see the whole of our group approaching the building together they might become alarmed.

My companion and I went forward, and on reaching the platform we had no difficulty in locating the chute, as we could see the bags being thrown down into it.

Without further delay we got onto the platform and made for the chute, to the extreme surprise of the post-men.

Bending our heads, we got in and shot forward. I was the first down, and I do not know how I kept on my feet, as the incline was about forty-five degrees and was not unlike a helter-skelter at a fair. When I reached the floor I was travelling at such speed that I had to run halfway through the building before I could come to a standstill.

Then I looked behind me. After me came my companions sliding down in most undignified fashion and tumbling on the floor when they arrived. They were quickly on their feet, and we made our way at once to the section where we knew the government mails were sorted.

The officials were taken completely by surprise. We had

them covered and with their hands up before they had time to realize what was happening.

The bags for the military, RIC, the under-secretary and other important offices were quickly collected, and we brought them to the chutes. We had a troublesome job getting them onto the platform. But we did it, and then quickly threw them into a waiting motor van which had been driven up for the purpose. We saw it vanishing round a side street as we made off on foot in a different direction.

When, later in the day, I called at our office, I learned to my surprise from the three intelligence officers who had entered the front of the Rink, that they were in the building and had had the staff held up for fully three minutes, suffering great anxiety, before they saw our inelegant arrival down the chute. The vice-commandant's watch apparently had been a couple of minutes slow.

CHAPTER XVI

The war had been intensified, and the British were making a determined and ruthless effort to bring our resistance to an end.

They could no longer get recruits in Ireland for the RIC, and drafts of 'Auxiliaries' and 'Black and Tans' were sent over from England to fill up the gaps we were making in that branch of their armed forces.

The Auxiliaries were recruited from ex-officers who had fought in the Great War. The Black and Tans were a mixed crowd of ex-soldiers and rough customers who were mainly attracted by the high pay which was offered for their services in 'stamping out rebellion' in Ireland.

They were given a pretty free hand in their methods of doing it. They were addressed from time to time upon their duties, and occasionally some extracts from these lectures were made public in spite of the rigorous censorship of the press. One superior officer, advising his men, said: 'The more you shoot the better I'll like you,' and Lord French, the Lord Lieutenant, expressed the opinion that the Irish should be crushed 'as you would stamp on a poisonous insect'.

It was necessary for us, therefore, to be prepared for the new offensive and to intensify our campaign also.

One morning I was sent to Ballsbridge Post Office to verify a report the D/I had received that a tender-full of Auxiliaries called there each morning and collected the mailbag consigned to the Auxiliary Division, stationed at the adjacent Beggars Bush Barracks.

I confirmed this fact, and reported that the number of Auxiliaries never exceeded five, that the tender arrived at the Post Office punctually at 9 o'clock and that I considered that the mailbag could be captured with comparative safety.

The director of intelligence, acting on my report, caused instructions to be issued to the local Volunteers to seize the bag, which they succeeded in doing after having made several abortive attempts, and without suffering any loss.

We went diligently through the captured letters, after making careful notes from them of the names of Auxiliary Cadets and their home addresses in Great Britain. This and other information we gathered in this manner was transferred to an alphabetical card index for future reference. Indeed, at a later date, this proved of much value in enabling reprisal burnings of Auxiliaries' houses in Great Britain to be carried out. These reprisals were taken only in the cases of those who had taken part in the sacking and burning of Irish towns and villages.

On the afternoon of the 13th October, while we were engaged in dealing with these captured letters, a knock came to the door of our office. There were three or four of us in the room at the time and, as we were wont to do, we got our guns ready while one of us opened the door.

It was the adjutant-general, Gearóid O'Sullivan. He was greatly agitated.

'For God's sake, lads,' he cried, 'take your guns and rush up to the Mater Hospital. The Auxies are raiding it, and Dan Breen is there. Quick! Hurry! And look out for Dick McKee who will be there waiting for you.'

Without further words we were on our way. It was only two days before that Dan and Seán Treacy had made their valiant escape from the Carolans' house in Drumcondra. In the middle of the night the house was raided by a party of Auxiliaries. After a fierce encounter, our men had managed to make their escape through the window of their bedroom. During the fight two officers of the raiding party were killed, when the raiders, in revenge, shot the man of the house, Professor Carolan, who had given shelter to our men without being aware of their identity.

Dan Breen, who had been injured in dropping through the conservatory beneath the window from which he had escaped, was lying wounded in the hospital, and his capture would mean his certain death.

Walking as fast as we could without appearing to be

running, my thoughts raced ahead of me in a thousand speculations. Would we be in time? Would he be dead? If so, would we be in time to avenge him? When I despaired, I found myself picturing the grins of triumph upon the faces of his enemies as they took toll of him for the loss of their comrades whose bodies were not yet buried.

Our thoughts feeding our anxiety, we had no heart to exchange a word. We covered the ground with great speed, but the way seemed interminable.

Passing by Nelson's Pillar we heard shots ringing out close by in Talbot Street. What could be happening there? I wanted to know, but our mission was of greater urgency, and my thoughts went back again to that question which was dinning itself in my mind. 'Shall we be in time?'

We had gone only a few yards beyond the Pillar when I saw a young man emerge from the Turkish Baths of the Hamman Hotel and approach a touring car by the pavement. Just as we drew up beside him he had the engine running and was making himself comfortable at the wheel.

I turned to my companions. 'Get in here,' I said, in feverish impatience. 'Here's a lift,' and I stepped in beside my new acquaintance in the front seat. Surprised at our intrusion he was about to make some remark when I interjected: 'Drive straight ahead, and go like hell.'

This startled him, but still he hesitated, till I showed him the handle of my pistol.

He was very unhappy. We had not travelled more than a hundred yards, when he showed signs of slowing down.

'Listen,' he said, 'for God's sake take the car and drive yourselves.'

The only answer he got was: 'Keep her going, or ——!'

In fact, none of us could have driven the car even if we had wished to.

On reaching a spot convenient to our destination we jumped out and, dismissing our driver, we threatened him with dire penalties if he mentioned us or our journey to anyone.

We hurried to the corner of Eccles Street. Looking up the street towards the hospital we could see that the crown forces had surrounded the building and that the search was still in progress. There were two armoured cars patrolling the entire block.

At the corner were a few Volunteers to whom we spoke. They advised that we should wait, all together, until the brigadier arrived. There was a public house at the corner and we went in for a drink. My throat was parched after our hurried journey. From the window we could see the armoured cars rushing by and our hopes sank.

In a few minutes we saw Dick McKee. Joining him, we stood at the corner and watched the activities up the street. He seemed greatly depressed. I asked him was there any chance of our doing anything.

'I am afraid we can do nothing now,' he said. 'I cannot allow the men to throw away their lives. But we will wait here, and if only the armoured cars will go away we will get a chance.'

He then told me the sad news that Seán Treacy had just been killed in Talbot Street, and of his own miraculous escape.

'I am only after leaving Peadar Clancy's shop,' he said. 'There were a few of us there – Peadar, Seán,' and he mentioned some other names which I have forgotten. 'Suddenly someone rushed in and said the Auxies were coming down the street. Seán was killed. He put up a great fight. There were others hit, also – passers-by. I don't know how I got away.'

Someone came up and called Dick aside.

The few sentences he had spoken to me filled me with horror. Seán Treacy was dead! That was the firing we had heard when we were passing Nelson's Pillar. Now it seemed certain that Dan Breen would follow him and we would have lost two of our greatest soldiers.

Hearing this news the Volunteers gathered round and pressed the brigadier to allow us to take action. Nothing seemed to matter now. 'We are being defeated,' I thought, 'but we must make a last stand.'

Dick was deaf to our entreaties and commanded us to desist.

Just then we saw the Auxiliaries leaving the hospital and entering the waiting tenders.

They were leaving and we had heard no shots fired! We could see no prisoners! I strained my eyes to search the moving figures in the distance. Could it be true? Had Dan escaped? We did not speak, not daring to give words to our hope for fear it would perish. We kept our gaze fixed on the enemy. They were driving away. Then sighs of relief escaped us at last. There *was* hope.

We had suffered a great reverse, I thought, but if they had missed Dan their victory was incomplete.

And Dick McKee was alive and with us! That thought gave me great comfort. I wanted to surround him with an invisible wall of steel so that nothing could hurt him. If we were deprived of his inspiring presence, then all would be at an end.

My thoughts were interrupted by Dick's voice, which had the power to draw me out of myself with one word. He was sending us away. There was nothing to be done.

The men started off in groups of two and three. Dick walked along alone. I was terribly anxious for his safety and could not bear to leave him. He had only escaped death by a miracle half an hour before. And here he was walking openly in the streets! I begged him to allow me to accompany him, making an excuse that I was going in his direction.

We walked along in silence. I could see that he was in great grief over Seán Treacy's death and was, in his heart, mourning for him.

When we reached Lower Gardiner Street he told me that he was going to his office. It was in a building occupied by the Typographical Society, and I knew that this was the brigade office, and I asked him if there was anything I could do for him, trying to linger with him, unable to tear myself away. He replied that there was not and promptly dismissed me.

It was now nearly six o'clock. Around the corner in Talbot Street I saw crowds gathered to look at the ghastly signs of the fight which had taken place there earlier in the day.

I bought a paper and read the official version of their victory.

Feeling very sad I turned my footsteps homeward, till I remembered I had now no home I dared to go to.

I must find somewhere to spend the night.

Chapter XVII

I had been now for three weeks 'on the run'. I changed my sleeping quarters each night, and I became anxious to secure a safe place so that I should not have to be moving continually.

It was by chance that a fellow Volunteer mentioned to me that I might like to join him and some others who slept in a dispensary on the north side of the city. This suggestion fell in very opportunely with my wishes. The relieving officer was a friend, and he allotted to us the portion of the dispensary which ordinarily would be his residence.

Dan Breen had not been captured by the enemy. He was not in the public hospital but in a private ward, and the hospital authorities had managed to conceal him from the raiders. As soon as the search was over he was removed to a place of safety.

The next day some Volunteers made a gallant though unsuccessful effort to capture an armoured car at Phibsboro'. Their plans miscarried and one of them was killed. I could never help becoming depressed over any loss of ours. We were so few in numbers that we could ill spare a single man.

On the Sunday following the death of Seán Treacy I

got word that I was wanted at one of our offices in North Great George's Street. Here I found the Squad, and we set out for Grattan Bridge, which crosses the Liffey near Dublin Castle.

When we arrived on the bridge we took up our positions. We had been told that two RIC men would pass by, and we would know them from a signal to be given by one of our intelligence officers who would be waiting nearby. They were known to this man, who would take out his handkerchief when he saw them coming.

While we were waiting we were within view of the sentry posted outside the City Hall. I saw that if we came into action we would run a great risk of capture, as it was known to us that the Auxiliaries were standing-to in Dublin Castle not a hundred yards away.

When we had been in position about a quarter of an hour I noticed two men walking along the quays in our direction. One was a stout, stocky man, with a red face. The other was tall and thin. Both men were in civilian dress with caps pulled down over their eyes.

I looked towards our intelligence officer. I saw him give the signal and point in the direction of the two men.

Before I had time even to leave my position and run forward, shots rang out. The smaller man was lying on the ground and the tall one was disappearing at great speed up Capel Street.

The minute the first shot rang out, from the hazard on the bridge an old hack came to life and started to race wildly along the quays. As we moved away I could hear the astonished 'Hike! Hike!' of the jarveys, whose interest had been diverted by something even more unexpected.

The dead man was a Sergeant Roche who had been brought up from Seán Treacy's district in Tipperary to identify him. He had gloated over the corpse of Treacy with such venom that a detective who was present was outraged and he reported the matter to our director of intelligence.

Chapter XVIII

It was Saturday the 20th November. The struggle was at its height. A number of Volunteers and civilians had been shot in their beds by members of the RIC and British Secret Service who were continually raiding houses during curfew hours.

One of their victims was Mr John Aloysius Lynch of Kilmallock, a respected citizen, who, as the custodian of the subscriptions paid in his district, had come to Dublin with £23,000 for the National Loan. He had put up at the Exchange Hotel. The place was raided between 1 and 2 a.m. by a party of British officers and RIC, some in uniform and some in mufti, who demanded from the night porter the number of the room in which Mr Lynch was staying. After their departure the dead body of Lynch was found lying between the sheets. He was not a Volunteer and had never carried a weapon.

Another man, Carrol, shot by the same party, and in somewhat similar circumstances, was the father of one of the Volunteers, and both these cases seem to have been ones of mistaken identity. It is assumed that Mr Lynch was shot in error for General Liam Lynch, OC of the 3rd Southern Division, who came from the same neighbourhood.

We had been engaged for the past three weeks locating the addresses of these intelligence men. Many of them were officers of high rank. They had taken up their abode in private houses in quiet residential neighbourhoods, where they lived in great seclusion, many of them under assumed names and occupations. By one means and another we had got upon their track.

At six o'clock I called to see a Volunteer who lived over a shop in Amiens Street. I had tea there with a girl with whom I had an appointment. She was a country girl employed as a maid in a superior boarding house in one of the fashionable streets on the south side of the city.

I was very anxious to have a conversation with Rosie, but I waited until we had finished our tea. We had met her several times already, and she had been able to give us some valuable information.

When I had first met her she had let fall scraps of gossip about her boarders which had aroused my suspicions. They were 'English gentlemen' she thought. They 'looked like military officers', though they did not wear uniform. They never went out during the day, but 'always at night after curfew'.

They were 'quiet gentlemen' she said, 'spending most of their time writing', and when Rosie had to clean out their rooms she was bothered by the overflowing contents of the wastepaper baskets which she had to dispose of.

She had, at my suggestion, brought me these waste papers, and on looking through them and piecing them together, with the supervision of Frank Thornton, a senior officer of the intelligence department, we had not been surprised to find notes relating to the movements of Volunteers and other data which were most interesting to us.

She had also managed to get hold of some photographs which were in the possession of these officers. They were of Volunteers who were being pursued by the authorities and who we had reason to suppose were on the list for summary execution.

By now we knew all we needed to know about Rosie's boarders – their names, both their assumed names and their real ones, their appearance, habits and the nature of their occupation. It had been decided that if we were to survive and our resistance to continue, the time had come to bring their activities to an end, and those of a number of other Secret Service men living secluded in the same way in other private houses in the same district.

Rosie told me that evening that life in the boarding house was just the same, but that two of her officers had moved to a flat in another street. I asked her had she heard the address. She had, and gave it to me.

Bidding her goodbye, I hurried to the office used by us

as brigade headquarters and found several officers gathered there. I was aware of the arrangements made for the following morning and gave my information of the change of address of the two officers.

I did not stay long as I had another appointment to keep. I went to Harcourt Street where I met a Volunteer officer whom I had not been acquainted with hitherto. I was to accompany him and his men on the following morning. We made our arrangements about meeting.

It was now near curfew and I hurried home to the dispensary. There were several Volunteers there, all of us engaged on the operations of the morrow.

There was no furniture at the dispensary beyond two double beds and a few chairs. We had our supper of tea and hard-boiled eggs, which we ate out of our hands, having no eggcups or spoons. We sat around the fire talking well into the night. I was wrought up, thinking of what we had to do the next morning, and I could feel that the other men were the same.

We were awake and dressed by seven o'clock. We breakfasted on the same fare of tea and eggs. I noticed that the men were examining their revolvers, seeing that they were in working order.

Outwardly we were calm and collected, even jesting with each other. But inwardly I felt that the others were as I was – palpitating with anxiety.

Shortly after eight o'clock we left the house, as we had a long way to walk to the respective scenes of our operations. Crossing the city we saw but few people astir, save an occasional milkman making his rounds. It was a beautiful, clear morning.

Coming near Merrion Square we passed several groups of Volunteers with whom we exchanged glances of understanding.

At Merrion Square I parted with my companions, and I walked on alone until I came to my destination. There I met the Volunteer officer with whom I had spoken on the previous night. He had several men with him who were waiting round the corner. He looked at his watch and said it wanted five minutes of the appointed hour – nine o'clock.

We had both received our orders. I told him what mine were: 'I am to get any papers in the house.'

Those were the longest five minutes of my life. Or were they the shortest? I cannot tell, but they were tense and dreadful.

Sharp at nine o'clock we walked up the steps of the house. Fortunately the door was open, while the caretaker was shaking the mats on the steps. One of our men held him up and warned him to keep quiet. (He was blamed for complicity, the poor fellow, and got ten years' penal servitude.)

We walked into a large hall which had two separate flights of stairs ascending from it. We divided into two parties, four in each, and as I went up one staircase with my companions I saw our other party swiftly mounting the other. The stairs were heavily carpeted and our footsteps made no sound.

On the landing were two doors which I knew led to the rooms of two of the Secret Service men. Here we divided again, and knocked simultaneously at both doors.

We identified the men we wanted. Each had a revolver at his hand, but our men were too quick for them.

Shaking, I said to the officer of my party: 'Wait for me. I have to search for the papers.'

'Wait be damned! Get out of here as quickly as you can.'

I was only too glad to take his advice. The noise of the shots must have been heard in the neighbourhood. We hurried down the stairs together.

In the hall three or four men were lined up against the wall, some of our officers facing them. Knowing their fate I felt great pity for them. It was plain they knew it too. As I crossed the threshold the volley was fired.

In the street I parted from my companions, they going south. I hurried along alone. The sights and sounds of that morning were to be with me for many days and nights, but for the moment my mind was absorbed with the matter of my personal safety. I could hear shots not far away and windows were thrown up and heads appeared. I was the only person in the wide, empty street.

'What's up?' was called down to me. 'Where is the firing?'

'I don't know,' I replied, and hurried on.

I thought I would never get across the city. Every moment I expected to run into lorry loads of troops which I knew would soon come tearing through the streets.

At Westland Row I came upon three policemen standing in a doorway. They did not challenge me, so I started to run. I could no longer control my overpowering need to run, to fly, to leave far behind me those threatening streets.

I was making for the quays below O'Connell Bridge. We had arranged for a party of Volunteers to commandeer the ferry boats, knowing that it would be impossible to cross by any of the bridges, which would all be held by the military.

I was out of breath when I reached the quay. There were a few other stragglers there, other Volunteers who, like myself, had had a long way to come. We saw the ferry boat landing with its party on the other side of the river.

It had just made its last journey!

We waved to them, frantically. They saw our signals, and to our infinite relief we saw a boat being rowed towards us. A few minutes more and we would have been lost.

Hurriedly we got into the boat and were rowed out into the river. I expected every moment to see the Auxiliaries dashing up to the quayside and opening fire upon us. I was greatly troubled thinking that I could not swim.

The boat seemed to go terribly slowly. I thought we would never reach the other shore, where I could get into the lanes and alleyways I knew so well.

At last we landed.

I reached the dispensary. My companions were already there. They told me that there had been a fierce fight between our men and the Auxiliaries in Mount Street, with losses on both sides. I longed to hear more news, and whether we had sustained many casualties, but I knew it would be too dangerous to be about in the streets.

Then I heard a bell ringing in a nearby church. It was the Angelus. I remembered I had not been to Mass. I slipped out and, in the silence before the altar, I thought over our morning's work and offered up a prayer for the fallen.

CHAPTER XIX

The English took immediate reprisals for the shootings of the 21st November. On the same afternoon, while a football match was in progress in Croke Park between the Tipperary and Dublin teams, Auxiliaries and Black and Tans drove up and, surrounding the football field, they fired on the crowd. Fourteen people were killed, including a Tipperary forward, and over sixty wounded.

On the next day, Monday, I got instructions to call at the house of a friend in North Richmond Street. I was to collect some papers which had been seized on the previous morning, and to bring them to our intelligence office for examination.

When I presented myself, the woman of the house brought me down to the basement and showed me a large black deed-box which, she told me, contained the papers I wanted. I had hoped that the papers would not be so bulkily packed, as there was intensified activity of the crown forces in the streets; and parcels of any size were always bound to arouse suspicion.

Having wrapped the deed-box in brown paper I set out, and got on to a tram going through Parnell Street. I put the box on the conductor's platform, and was relieved to be separated from it even for a little while, though I took care to keep it in view from where I sat.

I was just beginning to feel safe when I saw a patrol of soldiers holding up pedestrians a few paces in front of the tramcar, which now came to a standstill. I was seized with panic, my nerves not being at their best after my experiences of the morning before.

What will I do, I thought. Will I leave the box on the tram, disowning it, and try to get away, or will I stay and hope to bluff my way through? Either decision would bring serious trouble upon me. If I were held up with the papers in my possession, a horrible end was in store for me after a 'star chamber' interrogation, with torture, in Dublin Castle. On the other hand, if I lost the papers I would be court-martialled by my own officers.

While such thoughts were passing through my mind in the space of a few seconds, I found myself stepping off the tram with the box under my arm and gripping the pistol in my pocket.

Turning my back on the soldiers, I walked away in the opposite direction, stepping mechanically, without any hope at all that I could escape. I was like an automaton. I was, as it were, wound up to make those walking movements and would do so until I was stopped, but at the same time I knew that they were senseless and useless.

Then I found myself in a side street, and life and hope came back to me. Of my own will now, as if I were getting out of a nightmare in which I had been making movements over which I had had no control, I started to run. I was wearing a heavy overcoat, and I was soon covered with sweat, when, in a few moments, owing to the speed with which I travelled, I had reached my destination.

Curious to know the extent of my escape I speedily opened the box, to find my worst fears justified. It was filled with papers and documents belonging to some of the enemy agents who had been shot on the previous morning.

CHAPTER XX

On the night before the shootings of the 21st November, our brigadier, Dick McKee, was arrested, and I was never to see my hero again.

He and Peadar Clancy had been seen leaving Vaughan's Hotel. They were followed by a 'spotter' to the house in Gloucester Street in which they were sleeping, and after curfew the house was raided and the two men captured and taken to Dublin Castle together with another man, Conor Clune, who had been arrested in Vaughan's Hotel.

A day or two afterwards the three bodies, mutilated almost beyond recognition, were given to their relatives. They had been killed in the Castle in revenge for the Sunday morning shootings of the British Secret Service men.

On the following Tuesday or Wednesday, the 23rd or 24th November, I was sent by the assistant D/I to meet a detective named MacNamara. He was a friend of ours and had been working for Michael Collins for a long time.

I turned up at the appointed place – the Dolphin Hotel, which was quite convenient to the Castle. Standing outside the hotel I saw Mac, and it being dark at the time, and thinking he did not know me, I approached him and told him who I was. Immediately he recognized me, and it was evident that he had already been apprised of my name and description.

We walked together further down the badly lighted street till we came to a dark spot where any passer-by who knew the detective would not become suspicious.

Mac's first words to me were: 'Why have you got on that hat? The sooner you get rid of it the better.'

It was a black velour hat which I had only bought that evening. I had been rather pleased with it, but as soon as Mac spoke I realized my indiscretion. I never wore it again. Among the Black and Tans there was an idea that it was traditional for Volunteers to wear black hats – a sort of distinguishing mark by which they were known to each other.

We immediately got to business. Mac told me that he had not many minutes to spare. He had only slipped out of the Castle to meet me, and if he were missed the authorities might become suspicious.

'You know where to get Liam Tobin at once?' he asked.

'I do. He will be waiting for my report at Vaughan's Hotel.'

'Well, tell him we are raiding the Meath Hotel' (a few doors from Vaughan's) 'in an hour's time, and let them all keep out of Parnell Square tonight.'

Before I parted from him I asked him to tell me about the butchery that had taken place in the Castle on the night of the 21st. In that gloomy spot, standing beside him, I could see only the outline of Mac's face.

'You mean Dick McKee, Peadar Clancy, and Clune?' he said, his voice growing sad.

'I do.'

'Well, I heard that they had been brought in prisoners on Saturday night, and I had little hope for them then, and when I heard the alarm sounded in the Castle on the Sunday morning after the shootings, I knew it was all up with them. Such scenes! I shall never forget them. Cabs, taxis and hacks were rushing up all day filled with spies, touts and their wives, all in a panic, seeking safety.'

'But what about Dick?'

'The guardroom where they had put him and the others is just inside the gate, and the Auxiliaries' canteen adjoins the guardroom. I went into the canteen to see if I could hear any word of their moving the prisoners, so that I could send word to Michael Collins to arrange a rescue. In the bar the Auxiliaries were all drunk and thirsting for vengeance. Captain X— was there too. I had several drinks with them, but there was not a word about transferring the prisoners, and I had to listen to them cursing them with every foul name. I knew there was no hope, and I felt dreadful, just waiting for what was to come.'

'Well, Mac,' I said, 'they gave them a terrible death, I believe.'

'They did. Poor Dick was beyond recognition. I saw the battered corpses being taken away to King George V Hospital. They flung them into a van. I was nearly mad, and I had to act my part somehow. I had to look on while Captain X— pulled back the canvas screen to satisfy his hate with a last look. He flashed his torch onto poor Dick's ghastly face, swearing at him as if the dead ears could still catch an echo of his words, and at the same time hitting the body with his revolver.'

Mac then took leave of me, bidding me hurry along with the message he had given me, and reminding me of my hat.

I went on my way, my mind filled with all that I had just heard and my heart breaking, so fond and so proud I had been of our brigadier. I swore to myself that if ever fate gave me a chance of dealing with Captain X— I would be well rewarded.

I found Liam Tobin in Vaughan's Hotel and delivered my message. While I was speaking to him in the hallway, a tall, well-built figure passed by. It was Michael Collins. I caught only a glimpse of him. Liam told me he would see me in our office in the morning and, dismissing me, he hurried after Michael to a room at the back of the hotel.

CHAPTER XXI

The evening following my interview with Mac I called to Amiens Street to meet Rosie.

This was the first time I had seen her since the Sunday morning of the shootings, and I was very anxious to know what had happened afterwards at the boarding house.

The minute she saw me she burst into tears. This greatly surprised and distressed me. Putting my arm around her, I asked her what was the matter. This only caused her to cry more convulsively, so that for a while she could not speak to me at all.

'Oh, why did you shoot them?' she sobbed out at last. 'I thought you only meant to kidnap them.'

'But, Rosie,' said I, 'surely you know we are at war, and that these men were shooting our fellows?'

'I know,' she said, still crying, 'but it was dreadful.'

After a while she managed to calm herself and told me her story.

'After the gentlemen were shot, we were all terribly upset. Military and detectives arrived at the house, and they questioned us for hours. They took lorry loads of papers away with them. I was so upset I did not leave the house for days. You see, I felt I had had a hand in it, and I couldn't bear my thoughts, and at last I felt I must speak to someone. So I went to a friend of mine who was a priest and I told him everything.'

'Well, Rosie, what did he say to you?'

'He was very nice to me. He told me I needn't blame myself at all. He said that ye were fighting with your backs to the wall. "A defensive war", that is what he called it. He said the English had no right to be here at all. "Our boys must defend themselves," he said, and a lot more which I did not understand. He was grand and kind to me.

'Only, when I saw you, it all came back to me again.'

Chapter XXII

Towards the end of November, our friend the relieving officer told us that we would have to move. He wanted the rooms we were using for himself. But he was kind enough to arrange for us to occupy the upper rooms of a neighbouring dispensary, whose only occupant was an old caretaker named John.

We moved in to our new quarters without delay. Like our last ones they were quite unfurnished. But we were glad enough to get shelter anywhere, and as, of course, we paid no rent, we had no cause for complaint.

Old John received us without question. His manner was perfect in its calm acceptance of our arrival, as if it were an everyday occurrence for a number of young men to take up residence in an empty house and to bring with them neither furniture nor personal luggage.

He showed us our rooms. Then he brought us all over the building and through the waiting rooms where the poor people waited each day to receive free medical treatment. He led us out into the yard at the back, showed us the back gate through which we could pass in and out, and handed over the key to us.

Old John was about seventy years of age, and his snow-white hair and beard increased the impression of dignity which his reticence gave him. He seldom spoke to us except to answer some question, or wish us good morning. He never commented or expressed any opinion on all that was happening at that time. He did not know us by name, and addressed us collectively as 'Gentlemen'.

If I was the first to arrive at night he would inform me of the fact. 'The other gentlemen have not returned yet, Sir. The kettle is on. I wish you a good night.' That was all. And with a book under his arm he would retire to his room.

He never once asked us our names, or showed any curiosity about our business, or why curfew alone brought us indoors. At that time curfew had been put back to eight o'clock. It had been first fixed at midnight, but every time we brought off a successful coup against the enemy it was made an hour earlier. Perhaps it was with the idea of punishing the public, or rather with the hope of making us unpopular with them. But also, it had the advantage of giving the Auxiliaries and Black and Tans a longer period each night in which to prowl round in search of their prey.

Old John had a pipe which was hardly ever out of his mouth. This, with his book (on what subject I never knew), seemed to be the only companionship he enjoyed.

In his kitchen was assembled the only furniture in the house, so far as we knew. (We never penetrated into his sleeping apartment.) There was a large kitchen range, a fitted-in bath with hot and cold water, a table, a kettle, a few pots, cups and plates, and an enamel mug. These fixtures were all at our service.

The other rooms were empty except for an old chest in the room in which we slept, and which we put to good use. We filled it with supplies – arms and ammunition. The windows were curtained, and from the street the house appeared to be tenanted.

For the first few weeks we slept on a mattress on the floor. Then one night Liam shared our retreat, and he was so disgusted with his accommodation that he reported our forlorn state to Michael Collins, who immediately had smuggled into the house a few soldiers' camp beds.

My first companions in this dug-out were arrested soon after we had taken possession of it, and I was left alone. This did not suit me at all, and I mentioned my loneliness to two of the Squad who were also in need of a hiding place, and they promptly accepted my invitation to join me.

One of them was Joe Leonard, my comrade in the attack on the troops on the canal bridge, and the other was Jimmy Conroy, who had bought the paraffin to burn the Income Tax office.

Joe, as a very young lad, had taken part in the Rising and was imprisoned after the surrender. On his return to his native city he took a prominent part in the early activities of the reorganized Volunteers. He became an electrical engineer, but in the hard black hat which he invariably wore, and a dark raincoat, he looked more like a clerical student. Of an even-tempered, cheerful disposition, his frequent, rippling laugh was not unlike the rattling sound of machine-gun fire.

Jimmy was a painter by trade, and as a patriot he had been equally precocious. Before he was yet grown-up he had fought in the Rising by the side of his aged father. They were stationed together at Jacob's Factory. He had a simple, affectionate heart and a pleasing manner. Anything mechanical was interesting to him, and he was very handy and useful in all practical affairs. Except for a few months learning his trade at the Liverpool Docks, he had lived all his life in Dublin. He was a deadly shot.

Every night we returned to old John a few minutes before curfew.

We met usually in a little dairy shop at the corner of an alley, lined with small cottages, which approached the laneway by which we gained admission to the dispensary. I had been appointed housekeeper, and I bought our rations in the dairy each night.

Our suppers and breakfasts were always the same. Either tea and boiled eggs, or cocoa and bread and cheese. I was the only one of us who cared for cheese, of which

I am very fond, so that I offered it to my companions at our meals only as a polite formality. But on one occasion they took it, with the result that there was none left for me, upon which I lost my temper, saying: 'You did that on purpose. You know very well I have a passion for cheese.' I was chaffed on this account for a long time afterwards.

These two meals were usually the only ones we had, as it was very difficult to get dinner. It was too dangerous to go into one of the restaurants in the city as they were continually raided. Occasionally we were fortunate enough to run into a friend who brought us to his home and gave us a meal.

But there was one month during which I got my dinner every day.

Kevin Barry had been hanged in Mountjoy Jail on the 1st November. Owing to the jamming of his automatic he had fallen into the hands of the enemy during an attack. He was a medical student, and as he was only nineteen years old and very brave, with an attractive personality, his sad end had moved all hearts.

The nuns in a convent nearby had sent a message to one of our officers through an intermediary. They asked if they might be allowed to give dinner each day for a month to a young Volunteer 'in memory of Kevin Barry'.

The offer was passed on to me and I accepted it. The convent was very handy. I was not of course asked my name, or any questions. Everyone seemed to know instinctively the need for discretion.

The nuns called me 'Kevin'. It seemed as if they could not make enough of me, and I was welcomed every day with the warmest reception.

The Reverend Mother was quite young, with a very lovely face, and gentle, grey eyes. I used to notice her delicate, white hands. She was one of the two nuns who had permission to visit the prisons, and she was allowed to spend some hours with the condemned men on the eve of their execution.

With her great piety she was also an ardent patriot, and her two-fold faith must have helped to sustain her through the ordeal of those prison vigils. She had been with Kevin Barry and was with all our men, nearly all of them very young, who were hanged afterwards. Her faith – that they were dying for Ireland and were going straight to Heaven – was without a shadow of doubt, and she was able to communicate this supreme confidence to them. So that through her courage (I have been told) at those farewell meetings, there was no fear or depression, but on the contrary an atmosphere of gaiety and hope.

Our stay in the dispensary was most happy.

I selected the enamel mug, and the other boys used the cups. We chatted for hours, sitting before the kitchen stove each night. The kitchen, looking out on the back, was the only room in which we dared to show a light. The whole front of the dispensary was always in darkness.

When we retired to bed at last our room was illumined only by the rays of light from the street lamps. From our beds we could see the curfew patrols passing along the thoroughfare outside.

We slept lightly, waking often with a start to hear a lorry pulling up outside. There was a building opposite – Lourdes' Hall – which was often raided.

Even in our slumbers, the sense of danger was always near us.

CHAPTER XXIII

In the first week in December I heard that my home had again been raided, so I made a flying visit to find out what had happened.

My mother was surprised to see me and at the same time relieved to know that I was still alive and 'at large'. She quickly prepared a meal for me, which I greatly enjoyed, and she begged me not to stay long for fear I might have been seen and followed to the house.

'That is all right,' said I. 'I kept a good look out on my way.'

I asked her to tell me all about the raid.

'Well,' she began. 'We had gone to bed, when, shortly after midnight, we heard lorries coming down the road and pulling up in front of the house. I knew what was coming.

'There was a loud knock at the hall door, and I heard Emmet going down to open it. They kept banging on the door so that everyone in the road must have heard it. The next minute there was the noise of footsteps charging up the stairs. Our bedroom door was flung open, and a lot of men ran in, flashing torches on me. They must have found the switch, because the light was turned on immediately.

'There were fully a dozen men in the room. They gathered round the bed. One of them was dressed in a black uniform and seemed to be in charge. He was drunk, and kept lurching against the bed, pointing a revolver at me.

'Papa jumped out of bed and said: "What is all this fuss about?"

'They did not answer him, but told me to get up. Papa said: "You must clear the room first."

'This they refused to do, and Papa said to me, "Perhaps you had better," but I kept repeating that I would not, as I was feeling very weak.' (My mother had been suffering from heart attacks.)

'The other men in the room started pulling out drawers, and scattering their contents all over the floor. Some of them were wearing tam-o'-shanter caps (the Auxiliaries), and the others were Army officers.

'Well, while all this was going on,' said my mother, half smiling, 'Papa kept saying: "Do you know who I am?" and when they paid no attention to him, he said indignantly: "Do you know that I am a JP?"

'But they didn't seem at all impressed. Instead, they plied him with questions.

'"What are the names of your sons?"

'"Dermot," said Papa.

'"Where is he?"

'"There, in his cot."

'"What are the names of your other sons?"

'"Brendan," replied Papa.

'"Where is he?"

'"Inside there in bed."

'"How old is he?"

'"Thirteen."

'"You have other sons?"

'"Emmet, who let you in."

'"There is still another one, where is he?" and Papa replied that he was away in the country and that we did not know where he was.

'They ordered Papa to dress, and he did not even then realize that they were going to take him, though it was quite plain to me.

'He got into his clothes, and realizing at last that he was arrested, he said goodbye to me. They all trooped out of the room, with Papa, looking indignant, in the middle of them. I don't know how I didn't faint, as I felt quite dazed.

'I next heard the hall door being slammed, and the engines of the cars starting up. They had taken Emmet too, but they would not allow him up to my room to say goodbye.

'Before the cars moved away a shot rang out. My heart

stopped beating. But then Papa gave a loud cough and I knew it was a signal to me that he was all right.

'Two hours later the cars came back again. There were again loud knocks at the door, and Bridget got up and let them in. They dashed up to my room, as before.

'"Has anyone come in since?" they shouted, and again they searched the house, obviously thinking that you might have come home.'

My mother begged me to stay no longer and I decided, too, that it was time for me to go. Bidding her good-bye, I told her not to worry, assuring her I would be all right.

It was forty-eight hours after the raid before my mother was able to locate the whereabouts of my father and brother. They were prisoners in Collinstown Aerodrome.

The two of them became greater patriots than ever while they were there. My father appointed himself Chaplain, and gave out the Rosary every night, while my brother, making use of his training in France, spent his time drilling his fellow prisoners. When they were ultimately released, my father on the strength of his JP, and my brother on his services to the British Empire, they were both highly incensed.

When I reported the raid to Liam, the assistant D/I, the following morning, he told me he knew all about it. He and Michael Collins and one or two other staff officers were sleeping in a house overlooking mine, and had spent a restless and sleepless night with the enemy so near at hand.

CHAPTER XXIV

A few minutes before curfew on Christmas Eve, 1920, I was on my way home to the dispensary, and I called at the dairy to get provisions for our supper and breakfast.

Neither Joe nor Jimmy was there, and I waited, listening to a gramophone playing in the parlour off the shop. Then the clock struck ten, and I could delay no longer. I must get under cover and the shop must be closed before the curfew patrols came round.

When I got into the dispensary, I found that old John had the kettle boiling and a big fire burning in the range. He wished me goodnight and retired to bed.

I felt very lonely. I kept wondering why neither Joe nor Jimmy had turned in. I was so miserable that I took a hot bath and went to bed. But I could not sleep. I could hear people passing outside my window, singing. I thought they must be drunk to be defying the curfew regulations.

I found myself picturing the more happy Christmases I had spent, when, after I was in bed, my mother would be stealthily preparing my presents. So that when the joy bells started to ring out I felt very angry with the world. Never should I have thought it possible to have so sad a

Christmas Eve. Then I touched my Mauser pistol under my pillow and the feel of it gave me consolation. I had one true friend that would not desert me.

I must have fallen asleep, because opening my eyes I found it was daylight. There was no one to wish me a happy Christmas. I got up and, putting on the kettle, I thought, here is Christmas morning and there is no one even to prepare my breakfast!

I went out to a late Mass, and I was very pleased to meet Jimmy. He was surprised to hear that I had been alone all night in the dispensary and was sorry to have forsaken me.

After Mass, we went to an old stable owned by Jimmy's father where he kept an ass and cart for carrying around his paints and ladders. In the stable was a motor-cycle which Jimmy had captured from a military despatch rider a few weeks previously.

We got the cycle into running order and decided to risk paying a flying visit to my home for dinner. My family were delighted to see us, and I felt now that Christmas was the same as ever and I forgot my troubles.

We did not dare to tarry long in the house. Jimmy suggested that we should take a run through the country and I agreed, forgetting both the bad nature of the roads and the hardness of the pillion seat. But though my physical discomfort was considerable, our hearts were light, and when we got back to the dispensary we enjoyed that feeling of pleasant, half-somnolent weariness which comes at the end of a day spent happily in the open air.

CHAPTER XXV

From the time I became attached to the intelligence staff, I was kept very busy. Hardly a day passed without some important operation taking place.

About this time, January 1921, we had been very much occupied with the activities of a certain group of RIC under the leadership of a west of Ireland man whom I shall refer to as Nemo.

This group was composed of about twelve policemen from those parts of the country where the Volunteers were most active. Each policeman had been attached to the Crimes Special (Political) Branch in his district for a number of years, and had made it his business to know the political opinions of all the people in the neighbourhood.

The group had now been stationed in Dublin for some time. They patrolled the principal streets in civilian clothes, on the lookout for any Volunteer up from the country. They greatly interfered with the mobility of the Volunteers and were one of the most effective arms operating against us.

A Volunteer named Howlett on arrival at the Broadstone Station had been met by this gang and shot dead;

and this was but the first of a series of such acts committed under Nemo's leadership.

The D/I was most anxious to have this group ambushed, but it was a difficult undertaking as there was no regularity about their movements.

In January, a Volunteer from Galway named Tom Newell, who knew Nemo, came up to Dublin and was attached to our department to help us in our quest. Newell was a small, sturdily built fellow of about thirty years. His healthy complexion and his cap and the cut of his clothes betrayed him as being a countryman.

The Squad was now working in cohesion with the Active Service Unit.

One morning towards the end of January, while I was working on some papers in our office in Crow Street, Newell rushed in to say that he had just seen Nemo and his men going up Grafton Street.

Liam Tobin immediately took action. A messenger was despatched to the Active Service Unit, who were standing-to in a building close at hand, with instructions to them to proceed at once to Stephen's Green and there await orders.

I was told to go with Newell, and, when we had located the gang, to get in touch with the Active Service Unit and arrange that they should be trapped in one of the streets by a rapid movement of the ASU.

I thought that possibly the policemen were on their way

to Harcourt Street Station on the lookout for Volunteers from the country, bearing in mind their former action at the Broadstone Station.

Newell and I hurried along and were quickly in Grafton Street.

We were walking side by side on the crowded footpath when suddenly I saw two men approaching us. They were so near that I had no time to question Newell. I was at once alarmed. One of the two men was wearing a cap and the moment I saw him I guessed he was Nemo.

They appeared to take no notice of us. And we, of course, looked straight ahead. They passed without giving us a glance. And then, with a swift turn, they wheeled, and had us between them.

'Don't stir,' they said, threateningly.

We were unarmed.

The movement was carried out so quietly and neatly that the pedestrians did not notice anything amiss.

I could see that we were covered from their pockets, and looking around me I saw that we were surrounded. The gang were standing about in groups of two and three on either footpath.

Nemo and one of his men got Newell between them. Another of the group walked along with me. We were led into Suffolk Street, and the beating of my heart was nearly suffocating me. I was sure we were being brought to the

Castle. I thought of Dick McKee, and I thought I was about to share his fate.

I began an Act of Contrition, and I had no sooner finished one than I began another. I don't know how many I had repeated when, on reaching Dame Street, Newell and I were told to stand against the wall.

We were placed some distance apart.

We were cross-examined separately.

'What is your name?' 'Where did you meet the man you are with?'

I could not hear Newell's answers, nor he mine, but judging by the ugly expressions which came on their faces, they did not tally.

I felt that my time had come, yet I tried to bluff.

I said I was a nationalist and believed in Home Rule, and that if only they would bring me home they would find out the truth of what I said. I was thinking of the picture of John Redmond, the constitutional Home Ruler, which my father had hanging over the mantelpiece, and I imagined, like a fool, that before hitting me up they might go to the house to verify my story.

Then suddenly I heard Newell shouting: 'I know you, you dog, and you know me …'

He had lost his temper at last, sick of the lies he was telling, with his enemy standing before him and he unable to get his hands on him to give him what he deserved. He felt it was all up with him anyhow, as I did myself.

My own inquisition was over too.

'You can walk on now. Go to the right, and don't look back.'

I walked on, two of the gang following me. But how I kept to a walking pace I do not know. I wanted to spring round and face them. But what could I have done without my Mauser! I knew their game. It had become a way of getting rid of our men. They were officially accounted for as being 'shot while trying to escape'.

My knees shook under me. Mercifully, at first there were a good many people on the pavement. I might get a few minutes yet. 'To the right' was to the quieter streets. I began my Acts of Contrition again.

The agony was to keep walking. I wanted to run, to tear through the streets away from those footsteps pacing behind me. That was what they wanted too.

People passed me by as if I were walking the streets for pleasure like themselves, with no idea at all of the plight I was in. Over and over again, in anticipation, I was shot in the back as I walked along those interminable streets. I wanted to bend in my waist to escape the bullets, just as I used to do when I was a kid coming out of a dark room to escape from a ghostlike hand that might clutch me from behind.

I turned round 'to the right' into Trinity Street. There were fewer pedestrians and I walked faster. But yet I managed still to keep to a walking pace. Then I was round the corner of Andrew Street. Here it was still quieter and the footsteps behind me louder.

I could stand it no longer. I dashed round the next corner into Wicklow Street. A few paces on was the building in which my father had his office. For a moment I was out of sight of my pursuers, and in that moment I got through the doorway and up the stairs.

I was shaking. I was not sure that they had not seen me. I could not drag myself to the window to look into the street. I threw myself in a chair and listened for the footsteps coming up the stairs.

Minutes passed. I began to feel a gleam of hope. Perhaps I had given them the slip. I did not dare to ponder on this thought lest it should prove untrue.

I looked round the office and saw my father's typist looking at me in bewilderment.

An idea came to me. I jumped up.

'Put on your hat and coat quickly, and come out with me,' I said.

Still bewildered, she obeyed me. We went down the stairs. Linking my arm in hers, and not daring to look up or around me, we passed out into the street. Arm in arm, we walked up a side street to Stephen's Green like sweethearts taking an outing. Once there, I knew I would be safe with the boys.

At last, I dared to look round. There was no one following me!

I said goodbye to the girl. She must have been dumbfounded at my strange behaviour, but she asked me no questions.

I walked into Stephen's Green. I found my friends and related to them my terrible experience. They shook the hands off me, congratulating me on my escape.

But poor Newell! They asked me where he was, and I had to tell them I did not know. The evening papers informed us.

He had been riddled 'by unknown men' in Greek Street. But he was alive and in King George V Hospital, a prisoner.

They gave him a dreadful time there, trying to extract information.

After the Truce, Michael Collins got him handed over and placed him in one of the city hospitals. He was for two years on his back and came out of it a cripple.

CHAPTER XXVI

The day after my escape from Nemo I was instructed by a senior member of the intelligence staff to verify a report which had been received concerning Nemo. It was reported that he and his men lunched in the Ormond Restaurant on the quay, close to Dublin Castle.

I was badly shaken by my experience of the day before and I refused to obey this order, as I knew I would be recognized by them. I said I would go with a party of Volunteers and attack them, but that I would not go unarmed and alone, and become a voluntary victim of their campaign.

My refusal greatly angered this officer, and to bring home to me my insubordination, he arranged with the assistant D/I to have me transferred to a new office we had just secured over a Picture House in Great Brunswick Street.

I felt I was in disgrace, but I was satisfied that I had acted logically.

That afternoon we transferred a duplicate set of papers and some revolvers to a new office. With two separate offices, and duplicates of all papers, we could not be completely disorganized in the event of a raid on one of them.

In the new office I was unpacking the guns when a small automatic caught my attention. I was looking it over with great interest when suddenly, with a loud report, it went off.

I was dumbfounded, and hastily laying it down I felt a terrible pain in my left hand, which was pouring blood.

My companions broke out into a violent storm of abuse for my carelessness, fearing for the safety of the office which we had only just acquired. Only one lad, Paddy, did not blame me, but rushing out, brought me back a glass of brandy, which I immediately drank with great appreciation.

One of the boys got a cab from a nearby hazard to bring me to hospital. I was in great pain. I wrapped a handkerchief round my hand, and getting into the cab we drove up Brunswick Street, where, to my further dismay, the horse stumbled and fell.

I had to get out of the cab, while a curious crowd quickly gathered. I was a conspicuous figure, holding my hand in a now scarlet handkerchief. I am sure they connected me with an ambush.

I was most uneasy, fearing every moment that the troops would come on the scene. But with so many willing helpers the horse was soon pulled up onto his legs again and we proceeded on our way.

When I entered the accident ward of the hospital a doctor quickly put a first-aid dressing on my wound. As soon as he was finished he told me to clear off, as the military might be along any time.

'Wait now, a minute,' he said, 'give me some name or other. We are compelled to keep a register of people treated for wounds and are supposed to detain them pending the arrival of the authorities.'

I invented a name and address, and being urged again by the doctor to hurry away I lost no time in obeying him.

That evening I received a message that I was not to go near any of our offices till my wound was healed. Entering any one of them with a bandaged hand, I might draw attention to them.

I suffered great pain and had great difficulty in getting my wound dressed. I had to keep indoors for about a week, as to be held up by a patrol would be fatal.

Every second or third day, dodging any military lorries I met, I made my way to a friendly doctor, Dr John Ryan, who lived in Gardiner Street.

He dressed my wound, first running a steel rod through the hand to keep the wound open, as it had turned septic. This caused me excruciating agony, and as I have always been terrified of pain the ordeal tried me sorely.

After a week I had him put a small dressing over the wound, and putting the injured hand in my pocket (ignoring his instructions about carrying my arm in a sling), I returned to duty.

CHAPTER XXVII

Joe, Jimmy and I had retired to bed in the dispensary as usual on the night of Holy Thursday, 1921.

During the early hours of the morning we were awakened by loud noises outside. Peeping out through the curtains we were alarmed to see lorry loads of troops drawn up in the street.

Just outside our window a large tank was stationed. This sight quite overwhelmed us. Glued to the spot and shivering, undressed, we watched the soldiers. They were driving iron stakes into the ground, and putting barbed wire entanglements across the street. Then a field kitchen was driven up.

Now we knew! An investment was taking place. They were closing in our area preparatory to combing out every house in it.

Filled with consternation, we hurriedly dressed ourselves, and Joe went to see whether it would be possible for us yet to make our way out at the back. He returned to tell us there was a sentry in the lane.

From our bedroom, we could hear someone being halted. We listened to the voices. He was a baker going to work. They were detaining him.

It was now five o'clock. Curfew was over. We held a whispered consultation. We agreed that our only chance of escape was to try to make a get-away from the back. As it was, we were trapped and had to take our chance.

We decided that if we were caught we would try to bluff, saying we were milkmen and had to be out early. We left our guns behind to be able to play our part.

Noiselessly we opened the back gate and peering up the lane we saw the Tommy standing on duty, *with his back to us*. There was a chance.

The other end of the lane was a cul-de-sac, and without making a sound we tiptoed to the wall, hoping to God the sentry would not turn round.

We crossed the wall, and found ourselves in a back garden. We crouched down, waiting to hear a challenge.

None came.

After that, with hope in our hearts, we crossed several other walls until we came to an alleyway which brought us out onto the North Circular Road.

On the road, not a hundred yards away, we saw three tenders of Auxiliaries. They had been raiding a house and had not yet left it, so we made our way in the opposite direction.

We had not gone very far when we heard the cars coming after us. At that moment a hall-door opened and a postman asked us the time. Joe seized his opportunity.

Walking up to the door to answer the question, we saw him push the postman before him into the hall and shut the door after him.

Jimmy and I were now alone, and we hurried down the first side street we met and turned into a laneway. My heart was beating at a terrible speed, and, sure that we had been seen, we stood together listening for the sound of the approaching cars.

Then we heard them pass by, continuing on their way.

Exulting, we waited until Joe came along and joined us, when we made our way to my home where we enjoyed a hearty breakfast.

As soon as we had finished, we set out again to discover what was happening round the dispensary. We learned that they had drawn a cordon round the whole vicinity. The procedure was as usual. All the men in the houses were brought out and questioned and scrutinized by their intelligence men. Many Volunteers were captured in this way. During the three days that the troops remained in possession, every house was ransacked, and in some stables which were used as dumps by the Squad, large quantities of arms and ammunition were discovered, including a dump of Jimmy's.

These seizures greatly crippled us, as our supplies of ammunition and hand-grenades were very limited, and it had become well-nigh impossible to smuggle fresh supplies into the country.

When the investment was lifted and the troops had departed to repeat their activities in another area, we made our way cautiously to the dispensary.

To our joy and comfort we found old John safe in the house and quite undisturbed, just as we always found him on our return each evening. We had had no hope but that he had been arrested or shot on the discovery of the box full of arms in our room. To our surprise we learned, in reply to our questions, while as usual he volunteered no opinion, that for some unaccountable reason the dispensary had not been visited. It was the only building in the whole area to escape the search.

The house next to the dispensary (which was on the outside edge of the invested area) was used as their head-quarters by the military during their three days' occupation.

Chapter XXVIII

In late April 1921 I was instructed one evening by the assistant D/I to report to the Plaza Hotel in Gardiner's Row. This building was being used as the offices of a trade union body, and one of the offices was now our brigade headquarters.

When I walked into the room I saw several staff officers assembled. Among them was the director of intelligence, Michael Collins.

I knew Michael by sight, but this was the first occasion on which I met him face to face. He was sitting at a table and he gave me a friendly nod when I reported to him.

I felt very important to be in such company, but at the same time the presence of Michael completely overawed me. I was very vexed with myself not to be able to be at my ease, as I was most anxious to make a good impression.

He told me that the superintendent of the Corporation abattoir (who was also a Volunteer officer) had reported to him that an armoured car called to the abattoir each morning at six o'clock to escort supplies of meat to the military barracks.

'I want you to go to the superintendent's house,' he said,

'and observe the movements of the crew, and see if there is any possibility of capturing the car.'

Seán MacEoin was a prisoner in Mountjoy Jail. He was a fine and chivalrous soldier, having conducted the campaign in Longford with brilliant success and great humanity. But he had been captured after an ambush, and was awaiting his court-martial at which he was certain to be sentenced to be hanged. Michael Collins was determined to rescue him, and with the help of an armoured car there was a chance. I was to take up residence in the superintendent's house and to make my observations over several mornings.

The next night shortly before curfew I went to the house. The superintendent's wife, Mrs Lynch, was expecting me. Her husband, the Volunteer, was 'on the run' and very much wanted by the authorities, so that he was unable to sleep at home. The house was raided for him from time to time, which added to the precariousness of my position.

My hostess welcomed me warmly. She made me acquainted with her two young children, and showed me over the house. From the drawing-room window, which faced onto the abattoir, she pointed out the position usually occupied by the car.

It was moonlight, and, while paying due attention to what Mrs Lynch was telling me, my eyes wandered round looking for a possible way of escape in the event of a raid on the house. To my horror I saw something else – a sight calculated to strike far greater fear to my soul than the approach of any number of armed men. Below me, scurrying about in the moonlight, were shoals of rats!

I withdrew hastily from the window, making up my mind that, if that were my only way out, I would cheerfully allow myself to be murdered in my bed.

I was then shown to my room, which looked most comfortable and inviting, and after an excellent supper I retired for the night. Mrs Lynch promised to call me in good time so that I could watch the arrival of the armoured car in the morning.

She was as good as her word and, hurriedly dressing myself, I went down and took up my position by the drawing-room window. Kneeling down, I could see, through the lace fringe at the bottom of the blind, all that was going on.

I saw the arrival of the armoured car. It accompanied two lorries, and while it pulled up exactly on the spot opposite the window, only a dozen paces away, which Mrs Lynch had pointed out to me, the lorries were driven on up the yard to be loaded with the meat.

I saw the door of the car opened. Four soldiers got out. They were dressed in dungarees and each had a revolver on the holster of his belt. Lighting cigarettes, they stood chatting.

It was a double-turreted car and I knew the crew consisted of six men. On getting out, one of the soldiers had locked in the other two by fastening a small padlock on the door.

Morning after morning at six o'clock I took up my position behind the window and saw this performance repeated. The lorries, conducted by the armoured car, made several journeys with their cargoes of meat to and from the various barracks. While they were away I had my breakfast and made friends with the two children of whom I had grown very fond.

Every morning I made my observations and every day I reported them to Liam.

After a week I was summoned to another meeting at brigade headquarters. On this occasion we met at Barry's Hotel, a few doors from the Plaza, where to my surprise and gratification I again saw Michael Collins.

We sat around a table. Michael asked me to tell him what I had seen and what my opinion was in view of my observations.

I described the arrival of the car, the several journeys it made and the conduct of the crew. I produced a sketch of my own, showing the position usually occupied by the car when in the abattoir.

They heard me out without interruption.

When I had finished, Michael Collins addressed me.

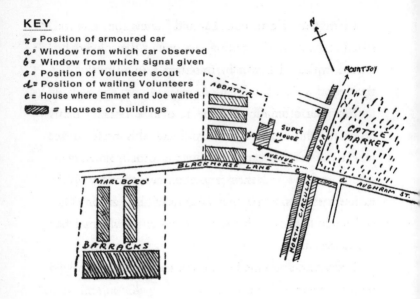

KEY

x = Position of armoured car
a = Window from which car observed
b = Window from which signal given
c = Position of Volunteer scout
d = Position of waiting Volunteers
e = House where Emmet and Joe waited
▨ = Houses or buildings

'I take it from your report you consider it possible to capture the car?'

'I do, Sir,' said I, 'but our success depends upon the exact arrival of our men at the opportune moment, which may only occur very occasionally.'

I had already explained to the meeting that during the dozen or so times I had had the car under observation only on one occasion did the whole crew leave it. Until such another occasion arose we could not capture it. When it did arise, it would be necessary for our men to be at hand to seize it instantly.

This seemed to satisfy Michael.

'Since they left it once, they will probably do so again,' he said.

He then addressed the others in turn.

He first questioned Pat McCrea.

Pat is a County Wicklow man, about forty years of age, an older man than most of us. He was out in the Larkin Strike and took part in the Rising, and was always to be found wherever there was any hard fighting to be done. Of a gentle disposition and charming manner, he endeared himself to everyone who ever had the pleasure of serving with him. Meeting him, it would not occur to you that he was a soldier, on account of the mildness of his address. Only, if you were observant, you might notice a directness in his glance which corrected your impression of his entirely peaceful disposition. He was our crack driver and took part in practically every action in Dublin.

In reply to Michael Collins's question, Pat said that while he had never driven a car of this make – a Peerless – he was sure he could get it to go.

I could see that his assurance was quite enough for Michael, who immediately proceeded with the rest of the business.

Two gunners had to be found, a spare driver and two other Volunteers to make up a complete crew.

Michael then unfolded his plans.

The car was to be captured by a swift and, so far as

possible, silent attack. This was necessary as the Marlboro' Barracks was close at hand and no alarm must be raised. The soldiers were to be held up while the car was driven off. The car would proceed from the abattoir to the North Circular Road, where two Volunteers would join it. These two men were my brother Emmet (whom I had introduced into the Volunteers on his return from the European War) and Joe Leonard, my friend of the dispensary.

Emmet and Joe would be ready waiting, each dressed in one of Emmet's British officer uniforms. They were to be taken into the car, which was then to be driven direct to Mountjoy Jail.

Michael described in detail the plan for gaining admission to the prison. He instructed Emmet and Joe in the steps they were to take – in their role of British officers obeying orders from Dublin Castle – to secure the custody of Seán MacEoin. He produced duplicate keys which he had had made from the wax impressions he had received from friendly warders inside the prison.

I listened with the keenest interest to this recital, observing with the greatest admiration the way in which Michael Collins considered every detail, explored every aspect of the job and overlooked no possible flaw.

Another meeting of the key men was held the following night, when final arrangements were made and last instructions given.

I returned to my post behind the blind.

Our plans for concerted action were now complete. The Volunteers, who were to hold up the soldiers and to seize the car, were to gather unostentatiously in the neighbourhood of the abattoir. One man was to lie concealed in a spot from which he could see the window of one of the rooms in the superintendent's house. From my vantage point I was to watch for the first occasion when all six men would leave the car. When this occurred I was to give a signal – I would raise the blind in that room which was visible to the waiting Volunteer. The moment he saw the blind go up, he would signal to the others who would appear at once upon the scene of action.

All of us were in our respective positions on the following morning.

But only four of the soldiers left the car and, greatly disappointed, I saw there was again no chance. As soon as the car had moved off, I slipped out by the back, and getting on my bicycle I made my way to headquarters. The waiting Volunteers, seeing me depart, moved away, knowing the job was off for that morning.

On the next morning, 14th May 1921, we made a slight change in our plans.

As usual, I was at my observation post at 6 a.m. When the car arrived I formed the opinion that the crew were in a not over-zealous mood. They seemed to be less vigilant.

That was my impression.

As soon as they drove off escorting the first delivery of meat, I made my way on my bicycle to a stable in Abbey Street which was used as a rendezvous and place-of-waiting by the Active Service Unit.

Here were assembled all the men on the job waiting for my message. Michael Collins was with them and I made my report.

MacEoin's days were now numbered and Michael, fretted by the continual delays and disappointments, was most anxious that the attempt should be made at once. I told him I was optimistic and thought there would be a chance later in the morning when the armoured car returned. I based my hopes on that appearance of carelessness in the mood of the crew.

Hurrying back to the house, once more I took up my position behind the blind.

I was not long there when I saw the car return. It drew up outside the window. I saw four of the crew get out and wander away through the slaughter houses.

They had not locked the door of the car!

I became excited and hopeful. With my eyes glued to the door, I wished with my whole being to see the remaining two soldiers step out.

For a whole ten minutes I waited.

Then I saw the door swing open. It had happened! I

had got my wish!

On stepping out, they lit cigarettes, and one of them shut the door, locking the padlock and putting the key in his pocket.

Nearly suffocating with excitement, I rushed into the room from which my signal was to be given, and *I raised the blind.*

That was the most awful decision I have ever had to make. Those few moments were the longest of my life, while I waited to see the approach of our men up the avenue which led to the abattoir. From that window I could not see the car. It was possible that during those two minutes the soldiers had got in again and I would see the massacre of my comrades, men whose places could never be filled, and feel myself responsible for their loss.

While I waited, I shouted to Mrs Lynch to get the children out of the way. We had arranged together that she should take them to a back bedroom, where they would be safe from stray bullets in the event of any firing.

Then I saw two Volunteers pass by the window. I recognized Tom Kehoe.

Dashing back to my post of observation at the other window, I was in time to see the two soldiers with their hands up, while our men were taking their revolvers. All my anxiety was now over. I was full of joy and relief.

The other Volunteers were scattering through the

buildings, searching for the rest of the crew, who had gone to watch the animals being slaughtered.

Our men were getting ready to take over the armoured car. From my window I watched Pat McCrea, with a benign expression on his face, struggling to get his legs into a pair of dungarees. The other members of our crew were doing the same, while the soldiers were kept covered. They had brought dungarees in parcels, ready. They were dressing up for their new parts. I saw Pat take the cap off one of the Tommies and put it on his own head. It was too small for him. He jammed it on his head anyhow, so that it had a rakish look, while he still struggled to get his foot out through the leg of the dungarees. I found myself laughing as I watched him, and I waited to see him search the soldiers for the key of the padlock and, finding it, unlock the door of the car.

I had now seen enough.

I ran upstairs to Mrs Lynch. I told her the good news. Then I locked her and the children into one of the bedrooms, so that, when the authorities arrived and the house was searched, she would not be suspected of any complicity, but would appear to be but one more of our victims.

At that moment I heard several shots ring out. It was necessary to be off.

Jumping on my bicycle, I hurried to the house where

Joe and Emmet were waiting. It was round the corner in the North Circular Road. They were ready, dressed in the British uniforms. I had just time to notice that they looked very well in them.

'Come on,' said I, still breathless with excitement, 'the car will be along any minute.'

They came out into the street. At the same moment the car appeared. We saw it turning out of the avenue and coming towards us.

I saw Emmet and Joe picked up. And then, the happiest young man in Dublin that morning, I cycled away to the stable in Abbey Street.

There I found Michael Collins waiting. His look searched mine for an answer to the question there was no need to ask. He was overjoyed, and my satisfaction was unbounded to be the bearer of such good news to him. He was all smiles.

'I hope the second part will be as successful,' he said.

CHAPTER XXIX

The next day being Sunday, I went to find Pat McCrea to hear the rest of the story.

I had already read the newspaper versions of the 'Daring Attempted Rescue of MacEoin', but I wanted to hear the true account. I was fortunate enough to find Emmet in his company.

Pat began: 'When we left the abattoir,' he said, 'I had a lot of trouble with the car. I only succeeded in keeping it in motion. I was afraid every minute the engine would stop running. I knew if it did I would never get it going again. There was no self-starter, and as the spare driver had not turned up there was no one available to swing the car.

'When I turned up the avenue leading to the prison, I was greatly worried to see how narrow it was. I did not know how I was going to turn the car in it and drive away again when the job was over.

'At the gates Emmet put his head out of the turret. A warder had come forward at once at our approach.

'"I have an important order for the governor," he said, holding an envelope bearing the letters OHMS in his hand so that it could be seen. "Open the gates at once to admit the car."

'The warder consulted somebody whom we could not see, and to our joy we saw the outer gates being opened. Then I drove in.

'I drove in,' repeated Pat, 'and I was unpleasantly surprised to see two more gates inside, barring our way. They shut the outer gate before they opened the two inner ones. As the sentry with his key opened the third and inmost gate, he said to me, "Will you be coming out again soon?" "I will," said I, while at the same time I turned round the car between the two inner gates, which were close together, in such a way that neither of them could be closed.

'Emmet opened the door of the car, and he and Joe Leonard jumped out, and I saw them, accompanied by a warder, disappear into the prison to see the governor.

'Tom Kehoe got out at the same time. There was a sentry standing inside the gate, and Tom meant to see that he didn't interfere with the gates.

'When our two British officers, Emmet and Joe, had passed into the prison, I thought I had better try and complete the turning round of the car in the narrow courtyard where we were, between the gates. I succeeded. I don't know how I did it. I know I could never do it again. Somebody was saying a Hail Mary for me, I suppose.

'There was yet the outer gate which was still shut. We had made arrangements about that; but if they failed, we were all trapped, as there was a sentry on the roof with a machine gun trained on the gate.

'Well, you know what the plan was, Charlie? Some of our men were to come with parcels, pretending they were relatives of some untried prisoners inside, but, really, to see that the gates were kept open for our escape, and at that moment I saw the warder open the wicket gate in response to a knock from outside.

'There, sure enough, was one of our fellows with a parcel in his hand. But the warder was in no mood that morning for a little friendly conversation to pass the time and he went to close the wicket again.

'I saw the visitor draw a revolver and with the help of two or three more of our men who were suddenly beside him, also with parcels (and also with revolvers), they held up the warder and, taking the keys off him, they opened the outer gate.

'That was a very happy moment, but my joy was short-lived.

'The sentry inside the gate had seen what had happened. He immediately fired on our men with the parcels, slightly wounding one and raising the alarm.

'As soon as the firing started, Tom Kehoe shot the sentry and at once I drove forward the car so that the outer gate could not be shut. There I waited, while shots were raining on us from the machine gun on the roof, until I heard one of our men shout, "Drive on! Joe and Emmet are on the back of the car."

'I did not need any second bidding. I "drove on" as I never thought I could have driven that car. The other Volunteers, who had been acting the part of the visitors, also jumped on behind; and I don't know how they were not all killed, as the machine gun kept up a continuous fire upon us the whole length of the avenue.

'Once on the North Circular Road again we were safe, as we were out of the line of fire. But we had not MacEoin. You know that.'

'No, we failed,' said Emmet, 'it was hopeless from the moment the firing started. If it could have been delayed for a couple of minutes we might have got him.

'What happened was this. It was plain sailing at the beginning. Joe and I followed the warder first through the outer iron gate, and then through an inner door also of iron. These were locked behind us. We were taken to the governor's office. It is just inside the prison, in the circular vestibule from which the corridors of the cells radiate. It was rather awful the sort of labyrinth we had got into.

'When we entered, we saluted.

'I told the governor, in my best English accent acquired in Flanders, that I had an order to receive MacEoin who was to be taken to Dublin Castle, while I showed him the forged order we had prepared. I thought it was all right, and that he would send for MacEoin to be brought to the office. But, unfortunately, he was not prepared to do so at once. He must telephone to the Castle, he said, to get our instructions confirmed.

'So there was nothing to do but to seize him, and we had him gagged before he had time to call out. Then, binding him, I told Joe to keep guard over him, while I would get the chief warder to take me to MacEoin's cell. I thought he might raise no objection, seeing I had just left the governor's room.

'But at that moment the firing burst out. The game was up. Fortunately the two prison doors were opened for us, our connection with the shooting outside not yet being suspected. Once outside we dashed through the courtyard. I saw a sentry lying dead with his rifle beside him. Picking up the rifle, we jumped on to the back of the car, which was now in motion and we got away.'

'What did you do with the car, Pat?'

'I drove it as far as I could from the prison, until I found we were on the Howth Road, two miles away. Here the engine stopped and I couldn't get it going again. It was a quiet stretch of road, and we stripped it of the two machine guns and the ammunition and set it on fire.

'We crossed some fields, where I took off my dungarees

and my Tommy's hat. I hid them in a ditch. Then we hid the machine guns and the ammunition.

'Our work done, we parted.

'I went back in to town to give a hand to my brother, Saturday being a busy day for him. You know he supplied Portobello Barracks with their provisions, and the first job he gave me, when I arrived, was to deliver a big order to the Auxiliaries' mess there.

'I thought he might wonder if I raised any objection, so I got out the van and drove it to the barracks. I found the gates closed. After a short parley, they cautiously opened them and let me drive in. They were taking precautions, they told me, "against a surprise attack by an armoured car".

'While I was delivering the goods, the Auxiliaries were all excitement.

'"What's all the alarm about?" said I.

'In reply they brought me into their canteen, and while standing me a few drinks, they told me in whispers about the terrible coup of the morning and that the car was "still at large".

'I felt very safe where I was, thinking of the fine alibi I would have in case of any trouble, when I suddenly remembered that I had left my collar, with my laundry mark on it, in the pocket of my discarded dungarees.

'I consoled myself thinking that there was little chance

CHARLES DALTON

of their being found. But I was mistaken. They were discovered, and I thought it best to go to Michael and tell
him.

"'Which is your laundry, Pat?" he asked me.

'I told him.

"'That's all right. I'll send along someone to see the
manager. He won't answer any questions. He will know
what to expect if he does.'"

They did not find the machine guns. When a suitable
opportunity came, we sent them to the country.

CHAPTER XXX

On the 21st May 1921 the Custom House was burned by the Dublin Brigade.

This was done as a necessary part of our campaign. It was one of the headquarters of what was left of the British civil administration in Ireland. Through their tax officials they were still able to continue to extract Irish money for the purpose of keeping the country in subjection, and it was therefore decided to destroy their documents and records. At the Custom House were kept not only those referring to Customs and Excise, but also the documents and records of the Local Government and other departments. All authority to deal with these matters of civil government had been transferred by the people to the National Parliament – Dáil Éireann.

To burn the contents of the Custom House in broad daylight, while holding up the large staff of hundreds of officials and clerks, was a big undertaking, and about 120 Volunteers were told off for the job. It was in the hands mainly of the 2nd Battalion of the Dublin Brigade, but all the men on active service were engaged for it, and also any Volunteers of the brigade who, while not whole-time men, could get off for the necessary hours from their workshops and offices.

No intelligence officers were engaged for this operation, but we were conversant with the plan of action.

At one o'clock on the 21st May, Tom Cullen (another I/O) and I left our office in Brunswick Street to have a look at the burning of the Custom House, as we knew that the Volunteers were to enter the building at that hour. Joe and Jimmy were both taking part.

Tom Cullen was a great favourite with us all. He came from Wicklow, and in him, Tom Kehoe and Pat McCrea, we had three splendid soldiers from that county, which otherwise played but a poor part in the fight. He had lived in Dublin for a number of years and was one of the two or three men most trusted by Michael Collins, and was his intimate friend. Though not yet thirty years old, he had a powerful physique, being fond of all kinds of athletics. He was a brilliant shot. His nature was cheerful and generous; he had nearly always a smiling, mischievous expression so that all who met him were attracted to him. He had a large heart and was immediately distressed by the sight of any poverty or cruelty. He loved Dublin, and knew every newsboy in the city, his ready sympathy causing him often to help them when they were in difficulties. So that they loved to serve him in return, were forever on the watch for him and kept him informed of enemy movements and the whereabouts of military patrols. His sad death by drowning in Lough Dan in County Wicklow in 1925 was one of the most cruel of our many losses, and deprived me of my most beloved friend.

Tom and I walked down the south quays to a spot from which we could see the Custom House across the river. There seemed to be nothing unusual happening and we began to wonder if the orders had been cancelled.

After about ten minutes, however, we noticed smoke coming from one of the upper windows, and while we were watching it we heard shots fired.

On the other side of the river we saw some tenders of Auxiliaries rapidly approaching the Custom House along the north quays. Immediately there were loud explosions and continuous firing, and we concluded that a Volunteer outpost on Butt Bridge was engaging the Auxiliaries.

The firing continued, and thinking the operation was over and the Volunteers safely retreating, we decided to hurry away as we had no business to be loitering round.

We started to run. The people were all standing in their doorways. Seeing us running they assumed we had been in the engagement, and shouted to us offering shelter and encouragement. Some women ran out and seized us, dragging us into their house, telling us we could get away from the back. We had trouble in convincing them that we were all right and had not taken part in the firing. They had made up their minds that we had been carrying out an ambush.

We walked on until we could cross the Liffey by the upper bridge. From the bridge we saw the Custom House in flames.

Later in the day reports came in which greatly disconcerted us. Six Volunteers had been killed in action, many wounded and about sixty had been captured.

This news greatly troubled us, as practically all the active Volunteers in Dublin had been engaged and it would be almost impossible to fill the vacant places in the ranks.

Jimmy was one of the men trapped in the building. Joe and I spent a very gloomy night thinking of the serious losses we had sustained. Of the original Squad, besides Jimmy, Tom Kehoe was a prisoner and Jim Slattery was badly wounded.

CHAPTER XXXI

The weeks following the destruction of the Custom House were very trying ones for us. Many of our best men had been killed or were in jail and it was necessary for us to conceal our crippled state from the enemy, who might otherwise have taken advantage of it to deal us a decisive blow. Ambushes were, therefore, carried out nearly every day by idle Volunteers, or those who could leave their employment for a couple of hours.

During this month, June 1921, I was introduced to two Americans. Two Thompson machine guns had been successfully smuggled in and the Americans had come to show us how to use them.

I listened to a lecture they gave to a few of us on the working of the gun, but it was purely theoretic, as the guns themselves had to be kept carefully hidden until the moment came to bring them into action.

The officer who was now in command of the Active Service Unit sent for me one evening and told me I was to go on an ambush on the following morning and that I was to operate one of the Thompson guns.

On turning up at the meeting place, I now saw for the

first time the two machine guns which were concealed in a waiting motor-car and I met the Volunteer who was to be my companion.

We drove to the position selected for the ambush and waited near a railway embankment. We had information that a troop train would pass by. A fresh detachment was arriving in Ireland from Silesia and was on its way to the Curragh.

We waited alongside the motor-car until we heard bombs exploding and the sound of gun-shot fire. We each took out one of the Thompsons and knelt down in readiness. As this was the first time I had the gun in my hand, it took me a minute to locate the various gadgets and, while looking it over, the train, badly wrecked by the bombing party, passed by.

It had been our expectation that, on being bombed, the train would be pulled up, when we could have entered into an engagement with the troops. But the engine driver did not even slacken speed and I failed to operate my gun, as I had not sufficient practical knowledge of it to get it working in the thirty seconds which the train took to pass our position.

The other Volunteer was more fortunate. He was in time to fire one magazine of twenty rounds before the train disappeared from view.

I was greatly disappointed not to have been able to use

the gun. Subsequently I was asked for an explanation and my opinion of it. I reported that it was satisfactory and that I would have been able to demonstrate its powers if I had had an opportunity beforehand to look over the mechanism.

Chapter XXXII

It was in the second or third week of June that I was summoned one day to brigade headquarters at the Plaza Hotel along with the other men of the intelligence department.

We were to co-operate on the following afternoon at six o'clock with a number of Volunteers in surrounding and holding up Grafton Street.

The plan of action was outlined to us. The Volunteers were divided into eight groups. Each group was to be accompanied by an intelligence officer. They were to converge on Grafton Street at exactly six o'clock, each group entering the street by a different side street, so that every person in Grafton Street would be hemmed in.

It was well known to us that at this hour the street was promenaded by Auxiliaries in civilian dress.

I had now made myself familiar with the Thompson gun, and I was told off to accompany two men of the Active Service Unit – Joe Leonard, my companion of the dispensary, and Bill Stapleton, a man of sturdy build and spirit, who had just learned how to drive a Ford car.

We were to proceed to the scene of action in a Ford

military van, which had been captured previously, and were to patrol round and attack any enemy cars.

On the following afternoon Joe, Bill and I went to an old stable where we found the van garaged and where the Thompson gun was dumped also. I examined the gun carefully and saw that it was in proper working order. I filled several magazines and left them handy in the back of the van. The van was hooded with canvas, and from behind the curtain at the back I could direct a steady fire.

Bill got the car ready, and from the difficulty he had in getting it started I could see that he knew very little of the art of driving. But what he lacked in skill in this and other directions, he made up for in self-confidence.

We set out at ten minutes to six, giving ourselves plenty of time to reach Grafton Street at the appointed hour. Joe sat beside Bill in front and I sat behind, facing the other way, with the Thompson gun on my knee.

When we came to Butt Bridge to cross the Liffey, Bill slowed up on account of the congestion of the traffic. As soon as we had crossed the bridge, Joe called out to me: 'Look out, and get ready.'

Quickly turning round I saw a patrol of soldiers right in front of us. I prepared to open fire and Bill kept the car in motion.

But when we drew level with the soldiers, to my surprise and satisfaction, I saw them waving us on, evidently taking us for crown forces from the outward appearance of our van.

Without further adventure we reached Duke Street, which enters Grafton Street midway. Here was our post, and Bill brought the car to a standstill.

It was now six o'clock, and we waited anxiously to hear the firing begin, while we kept on the lookout for the approach of any military lorries. From the car I saw three armour-plated lorries, filled with Tommies, pass down Dawson Street (outside the area of our operations). They were apparently going on a raid, as they continued on their journey.

At five minutes past six we heard shots being fired in Grafton Street.

We got ready for action. Bill had the engine running, and we were ready to engage any car we saw approaching.

The minutes passed and nothing happened. We heard no more sound of gunfire and there was no sign of the enemy.

At last we decided it was useless and dangerous to wait any longer. Bill turned the van and we started to drive away. All hope of an engagement over, we were not very happy in our position, with our barely concealed Thompson gun beside us and the chance of being held up likely at any moment.

We turned round the corner into Dawson Street at a

very sharp angle and as we did so I felt a severe bump. The bumping continued and the van was wobbling all over the street. Bill kept it going until we drew round into the next block – Kildare Street – where it came to a standstill. Aghast at this mishap, I jumped out and saw that a front and rear tyre were gone. There we were, stranded in a busy thoroughfare!

Bill could not get the car started again. We all got out and began to shove. By a great effort we succeeded in pushing it into a laneway. There were several unoccupied cars parked on the street, but not one of them was a Ford. Nor was there a driver whom we could have coerced to get us away.

But in the lane we discovered a stable which was un-locked. We pushed the van into it and shut-to the door. I noticed a blue document nailed to the entrance. It was a notice by the Borough Surveyor ordering the stable to be pulled down 'within seven days'. I wondered how many of the seven had elapsed.

We had to abandon our guns as well as the van, praying they would not be discovered before morning. It was now getting on for seven o'clock and the streets would be alive with troops. It was dangerous to be lingering.

We walked to the Shelbourne Hotel and, seeing a hack outside, we engaged the jarvey to drive us, directing him by a route in the opposite direction from Grafton Street.

We decided not to report our loss. We went to the dispensary, where we all spent a sleepless night. I thought morning would never come, so consumed with anxiety I was for the safety of our arms, now, owing to their scarcity, of such paramount importance to us.

Very early Bill was up and out to get two new tyres. He made his way with them to the stable, which had not been demolished in the meantime, fitted them on and drove away the precious cargo to safety.

We learned that the attempted hold-up had not been a success. Only two of the groups had been able to make their way to the street in time. These engaged some Auxiliaries, two of whom were killed. The other groups all encountered military foot patrols and were unable to get to their respective positions.

CHAPTER XXXIII

On Sunday morning, 26th June, Joe and I walked down to Howth to get Mass. We had spent the night happily with some Volunteers who had rented a cottage on the summit of Ben Eadar.

It was a peaceful, sunny morning, and the little fishing town was crowded with people who had come out from the city to enjoy the sea air.

We walked down towards the harbour. On our way we met a newsboy carrying a placard. Almost snatching a paper from him, we tore it open.

'Letter from Lloyd George to De Valera Calling a Conference.'

'Truce to be Arranged Immediately.'

We could not believe our eyes. I thought maybe it was a joke, or a trap to catch us off our guard. But we decided to hasten into town and find out the truth.

In the city we met some of our comrades who assured us that the news was authentic. We continued, however, to move about with our usual caution as there had been no Cease Fire Order issued by either side.

Immediately we got into touch with our superior

officers and put in a request for leave. This was granted.

We were in such a state of excitement and exultation that we could do nothing but grin and make over and over again the same remarks. We could not settle to anything. We kept running round, meeting and re-meeting, and always repeating the same exclamations.

We spent the whole week preparing for our holiday, though, in fact, we did very little. Our preparations consisted mainly in talking about it and anticipating its pleasures.

It was so wonderful a thing – to go away from all the fear and danger, and the hunted life, into freedom and leisure, that it took a whole week for us to prepare ourselves for such a change.

We had decided on the Isle of Man as a place in which we could find an atmosphere sufficiently unrestricted. We hardly slept at all on the Sunday night, 3rd July. Boldly, we had ordered a taxi to be at the dispensary at eight o'clock the next morning. While I was dressing I realized that it was the 4th of July – Independence Day in America. It seemed a good omen.

We were out through the door before the driver had time to knock. There were Joe, Bill and Jim Slattery of the Squad, or Active Service Unit, and Joe Dolan and myself of the intelligence staff. Jim was bandaged up, having lost an arm as a result of the wound he received at the Custom House.

We drove to Westland Row Station in the highest spirits. I did not feel any longer that I was in the world of everyday things. There seemed a radiance.

We took tickets for Liverpool.

As we were about to get on the boat we saw some Auxiliaries standing at the gangway scrutinizing the passengers. We mingled amongst the crowd, anxiously, fearing disaster on account of Jim's bandages. I was on tenterhooks until the boat started. It seemed hours until a siren was blown and she pulled out from the pier.

Then we could hold ourselves in no longer. Looking straight towards the Auxiliaries we raised a cheer. They could not stop us now.

This was my first voyage and fascinated with the ship I set out to explore it. In the dining saloon I found writing tables with notepaper and postcards bearing a picture of the ship. Delighted, I sat down and wrote postcards and letters to a large number of my friends and relatives. I thought of how they would envy me, and I pitied everyone who was not, like myself, on a mailboat making a journey into the unknown.

At Holyhead we were directed by a porter to a train that would take us to Liverpool. When I saw the train, I stood still in amazement. It was painted cream. It was quite unlike our trains at home. This had the greatest effect upon me in making me realize fully the joy of liberty. I was in a new country and had left behind everything that was a danger and a terror to me.

We reached Liverpool at about three o'clock. We took a taxi to the house of a friend whose address had been given to us. He welcomed us warmly and asked us what were our plans. We told him that we were going to the Isle of Man.

He came with us into the city and booked rooms for us in a hotel for the night. There was a boat leaving for Douglas at 10.30 the next morning.

We spent the evening looking round Liverpool, and when we could remember that we need not look at every passer-by in the light of a possible enemy, we wondered at the change in our situation. We went to a theatre and laughed immoderately at the not very humorous antics of a comedian. I envied the people of Liverpool their peaceful life, fancying they must be some special favourites of Providence.

When we went to bed it was almost impossible to realize that we need not talk in whispers. We turned on all the electric lights. We pulled up the blinds, wishing the whole world outside to see the glare in which we dared to reveal ourselves.

Perhaps that waking-up the next morning was the best of all – the slow, gradual realization of our new happy circumstances.

We decided to have breakfast in bed, to sample every

luxury and to do all things contrary to what we were accustomed hitherto.

I pressed a bell. A maid appeared and I gave an order. And it was a good breakfast! We could not stop laughing.

'What would they say at home to see us now? What are they doing?'

But we did not want to think of home.

When we got to Douglas we took rooms in a private hotel – the Broadway. The landlady told us that all guests must be in by eleven o'clock.

We were delighted with Douglas. But then any place outside Ireland would have delighted us. We bought flannel trousers, cigarette holders and walking sticks. We swaggered about, drawing attention to ourselves – tasting to the full our emancipation from everything furtive, cautious and retired. We spent our evenings on the helter-skelter and the switchbacks. We had our photographs taken. We hired a car and drove round the island, which I admired extremely. And, of course, we took no notice of the rules of the establishment, but roamed the streets till the early hours of the morning. To be out during curfew! To meet no patrols! Never, never could we get used to the delight of that experience.

We were able to get the *Irish Independent* each morning. We read that a Truce was signed on the 11th July.

And when I read that announcement, suddenly Douglas

had no more charm for me. I was no longer interested in the island. Dublin and home called me once more. I said goodbye to my companions and took the first boat that sailed from the island direct for home. As we drew near the North Wall I was moved with far deeper feelings than those which I had carried with me on departing.

I saw our tricolour flag waving from every window. I am not going to describe my emotions. I felt like a kid, a lump in my throat, trying not to burst out crying.

I jumped on a car. I bade the jarvey drive me through all the principal streets of the city. Dublin! The city was *en fête*. Flags everywhere! Could it be old Dublin!

I went home and enjoyed a warm reunion with my family.

But I could not stay indoors. I was restless. Again I wanted to see everything.

I went out, wandering through the streets. Unbelieving, blissful!

Bureau of Military History, 1913–21

Witness Statement 434

Charles Dalton

Member of 'F' Company 2nd Battalion
Irish Volunteers, 1917–.
Member of Intelligence Squad 1920–.

Subject
Activities of 'F' Company 2nd Battalion
1917–1921;
Intelligence Squad 1920.

Publisher's Note: All spelling, capitalisation and punctuation have been left as in the original.

STATEMENT BY CHARLES DALTON (Colonel, retired)

86 Morehampton Road, Donnybrook, Dublin.

I joined the Volunteers, F/Company, 2nd Battalion, in December 1917. My company officer at that time was Frank Henderson. Henderson afterwards went up to the battalion and Oscar Traynor then became company captain.

After some preliminary company jobs, I was sent for by the brigadier, Dick McKee, and attached to the H.Q. Squad on an assisting basis.

THE INTELLIGENCE SQUAD.

After participating with the squad in the seizure of the Castle mails at Dominick St., Dublin, in February 1920, I was again sent for by the brigadier who asked me would I join the G.H.Q. Intelligence Unit, which I did. I reported for duty to the Deputy Director of Intelligence, Liam Tobin, at an office in Crow St. which was used as our headquarters.

My duties were outlined to me by the Assistant Director of Intelligence, who was in daily communication with Michael Collins. They consisted of tracing the activities of enemy agents and spies, keeping records of enemy personnel, contact with friendly associates in government and Crown service, organising and developing intelligence in the Dublin Brigade as an adjunct to headquarters Information Service, and participating in active service actions arising from our duties.

Our Department was strengthened from time to time by the inclusion of selected officers, and, with the growth of duties and the increase of activities by the Crown forces, it was later found necessary to set up an additional office to house the Intelligence Department. This office was located over the Brunswick St. Cinema.

In those years of activity, the sources of our information were very limited, due to the fact that all Government Civil Servants, including the members of the Metropolitan Police, R.I.C. and other Crown forces, had taken an oath of loyalty to the Crown. The fact that they occupied pensionable positions, even though they had mild national leanings, did not induce them to be of help to the Republican movement.

One of the most fruitful sources of information to our Department would have been the Post Office, which controlled the delivery of correspondence throughout the country, the dispatch of all telegrams and the working of the telephone system. In those days the Crown forces depended mainly for inter-communication on the telephone and telegraph systems. We possessed the key to the R.I.C. code, which was changed monthly. Through this channel we were able to forestall Crown forces' raids, impending arrests, etc., but, due to the fact that our helpers in this department were so few, the results obtained were far from complete. Similarly, in the postal dispatch departments and letter sorting offices, we had very few helpers, and, although the members of the Crown forces used the mails freely, the amount of information gathered through interception, raids on mails, etc. was rather limited, due to lack of co-operators. In the Central Telegraph Office, Liam Archer, and in the principal Sorting Office, Paddy Moynihan (nom-de-plume 118) were the most important aides.

The Post Office aides invariably left their information for Michael Collins's perusal at addresses in Parnell Street, viz: Jim Kirwan, publican, Knocknagow dairy shop, and Liam Devlin, publican. They were the principal rendezvous for these people.

Before leaving the subject of postal assistance, it is well to mention that the Director received valuable information from some postal officials he personally dealt with who were engaged on the mail boats, and from London through Sam Maguire, who was in charge of that city on his behalf.

Amongst the important information that was supplied were particulars of the Castle mails, including Lord French's mails and how they were transmitted, and the plan of the Sorting Office in the Rink, from which Government mails were subsequently seized. In certain cases, copies of telegrams in code were forwarded to us, and in some instances, letters going to a particular individual who was a suspect came into our hands likewise.

COUNTER INTELLIGENCE.

Counter Intelligence was organised traditionally through the police. In Dublin city the 'G' Division controlled all political information, and in the country the Special Crimes Branch of the R.I.C. did likewise. In addition to these two sources of information, the British army had a military Intelligence Service which was conducted in Dublin by Major S.S. Hill Dillon. During 1921, the British Secret Service established an independent Intelligence Unit principally in Dublin, which worked, it is believed, directly with the Cabinet in London through the War Office. Agents of the latter body were identified by us, as these lived as civilians in the City, following fictitious occupations and participating, to a limited degree, in what was their final objective – the elimination of active I.R.A. leaders through secret murder. Many of these Agents were executed on 21st November 1920, before their operational plan was put into effective action.

In Dublin the 'G' Division operated with open contempt for the Volunteers until some of their members had been shot. After these shootings 'G' Division were 'confined to barracks' in the Castle and were thus immobilised from active detection work.

In this body there were two or three officials who co-operated with our Department and supplied valuable information to counteract the activities of the Crown forces. These were Jim McNamara, David Neligan, whom I met frequently and Ned Broy, whom Collins himself met. These men had channels of contact through very reliable intermediaries. In many instances, I or another member of our staff had, at short notice, to meet them adjacent to the Castle in the street. There we learned of intended raids, the location of prisoners, etc. The assistance of those men cannot be sufficiently recognised, due to the fact that they alone were able to confirm beyond doubt the activities of suspects whom we had under observation.

The Director of Intelligence was in touch with contacts in the prison service, warders in Mountjoy Jail – Daly and Peter Breslin. In the R.I.C. he received valuable intelligence from Sergeant McCarthy, stationed in Belfast in the County Inspector's office.

In the Auxiliary Division of the R.I.C. we had assistance from an Englishman, Sergeant Reynolds of 'F' Coy. stationed in Dublin Castle. He supplied information through a friend of his, Bríghid Foley, whom he first met during a raid.

As regards the R.I.C., this Force did not operate

in the city of Dublin, but a few friendly members were contacted in the counties where they were stationed. Their headquarters were located at the Depot, Phoenix Park.

The British Military Intelligence Department operated from the Dublin District office at Royal Barracks. Contact was never established with this body other than through the efforts of a typist, Miss Mernin, at a late stage in the struggle.

From the Intelligence Officer of the 1st Southern Division (Florrie O'Donoghue) copies of radiograms intercepted were forwarded to our office for decoding, but, as all these were in the British Naval numerical code, we were unsuccessful in decyphering [*sic*] them until after the Truce.

In Dublin city at any rate, the main sources of information to the Castle, in addition to police reports, were anonymous letters, telephone calls which we were unsuccessful in intercepting, and material supplied from what was known as the loyalist element.

The 'G' Division depended, as also did the Secret Service, for much of their information on particulars supplied, mainly about individuals, by newsvendors, hotel porters, policemen, as well as the ordinary police reports. For instance, Barton of the 'G' Division was held in the highest esteem by the publicans, pawnbrokers and other commercial men, due to the fact that he had established a unique method in the tracing of petty larceny and illegal pawning of stolen goods. In carrying out his routine police duties, he had many newsvendors and minor thieves of the pickpocket variety in his power, and he utilised this type of informer for checking up on the movements of prominent wanted Volunteers. After Barton's demise, informers of this type were contacted by other members of the counter Intelligence Service, and became commonly known as 'touts'. It was one of these 'touts', Pike, who followed Dan Breen and Sean Treacy from Fleming's of Drumcondra to Fernside, and it was another of these, 'Chanters' Ryan, who successfully discovered the hideout during curfew hours, of Dick McKee and Peadar Clancy, from which they were taken prisoner and subsequently shot. At the time of this occurrence, Ryan was serving as a military policeman, but lived in a disreputable neighbourhood in Dublin.

TYPE OF CONTACTS.

Outside those already referred to, the services of friendly waiters, hotel porters, railway officials and, in fact, anyone in a position to supply or confirm information relative to the activity of Crown agents was solicited and utilised. In this connection the elimination of spies was assisted through the medium of reports thus received. This type of helper was contacted by members of our staff. In reality, the number of dependable assistants in this category was strictly limited. The receipt of information was important, but more important still was the necessity for complete silence on the part of our informants, as failure to observe this would have frustrated the work of our Department, as well as possibly leading to the elimination of ourselves. Offers of assistance were many, but the integrity and resourcefulness of the would-be informants in many cases did not qualify them for inclusion in our network of helpers.

If, as a result of information supplied by a hotel aide, shooting accrued, this individual, as well as other members of the hotel staff, was subject to a 'grilling' by the Crown forces. Anyone known to have sympathies with Sinn Féin would receive special attention by the Authorities. Such an examination could possibly result in the informant double-crossing us, with unhappy results.

When we got offers of assistance we first had to make up our minds whether we could trust them or not, and then we could only tell them very little. There was the danger that, in their enthusiasm to give information, they would go and ask other people for information without exercising proper caution.

One of our greatest sources of information in the tracing of movements of prominent personages was the society columns of newspapers, covering banquets, dinners, etc. Also 'Who's Who', which enabled us to trace the clubs, hobbies, etc. of these people, as well as Press photographs taken at Castle or similar functions. In our Crow St. office we kept an alphabetical card index of all known enemy agents, Auxiliary Cadets, R.I.C. men, etc. Any information as to their movements, whereabouts or intentions obtained from the Press in this manner was tabulated and circulated to the country Volunteers, if it concerned them. Photographs were studied by our staff, and in many instances our identification, on the street or elsewhere, of these individuals was made possible through a study of their photographs.

G.H.Q. PERSONNEL, CROW ST. AND LATER BRUNSWICK STREET.

Michael Collins was Director of Intelligence. He operated from his own personal office in the daytime and saw his lieutenants at night. Liam Tobin was Deputy D.I., and Tom Cullen was Assistant D.I.

The staff consisted of Frank Thornton, Joe Dolan, Joe Guilfoyle, Paddy Caldwell (later transferred to 'An t-Oglach' staff), myself, Frank Saurin, Charlie Byrne, Peter McGee, Dan McDonnell, Ned Kellegher, James Hughes, Con O'Neill, Bob O'Neill, Jack Walsh and Paddy Kennedy.

Jimmy Murray was, I believe, a member of 6th Battalion and acted as Battalion I.O. Murray resided in Kingstown and was at one time employed on the boats.

Shortly before the Truce, Murray and Dan McDonnell were our contacts with Dave Neligan, who was then residing with another Secret Service man (Woolley) in Kingstown, having left the 'G' Division, on the instructions of Michael Collins, to join the British Secret Service proper.

THE DIRECTOR OF INTELLIGENCE AND HIS STAFF.

During the daytime Michael Collins worked from an office of his own, and at no time did he visit the Crow St. or Brunswick St. offices. Inter-communication was maintained by his special messenger, Joe O'Reilly. In the evening time Michael Collins used to meet Liam Tobin and Tom Cullen at one of his numerous rendezvous in the Parnell Square area – these were Jim Kirwan's, Vaughan's Hotel and Liam Devlin's.

In the earlier years Michael Collins used to meet these men at 46 Parnell Square and at McCarthy's in Mountjoy St. They were all on the run and on many occasions they stayed together, sometimes at Joe O'Reilly's lodgings, Smith's of Lindsay Road, and on other occasions at Paddy O'Shea's house in Lindsay Road.

Michael Collins used as his personal office Miss Hoey's house in Mespil Road; also Mary St., and finally Harcourt Terrace. I was on duty at the Harcourt Terrace office, which was an ordinary dwelling-house, furnished as such, and in the front bedroom the D.I. had his papers. These were concealed in a secret cupboard on the landing, in which he himself could take refuge should the house be raided while he was in occupation.

It was from his personal office that Michael Collins dealt with all the Brigade and country Intelligence reports.

ENEMY AGENTS AND SPIES.

Following the death in action of Sean Treacy, we received information through our contacts in the Special Branch in the Castle that Sergeant Roche and Constable Fitzgerald were in Dublin. They had come to Dublin from Tipperary to identify the remains of Treacy, and, evidently, to be available, if required, in the search for Dan Breen who had escaped, wounded.

On 17th October 1920, I was in touch with Dave Neligan, who told me that the wanted men would probably be dining in the Ormond Hotel that day, having left the Castle to do so. Neligan first arranged that he would take them to lunch and would indicate to me that they were the wanted men. Something went wrong with this arrangement, but nevertheless, the squad took up positions around Grattan Bridge. Neligan came along on his own and bumped into the two R.I.C. men who had left the Ormond and were on their way back. He conversed with them, and after parting from them, he gave the pre-arranged signal by waving his handkerchief. Those of the squad nearest to the R.I.C. men opened fire on them, fatally wounding Roche, but Fitzgerald escaped by running up Capel Street. Both men were wearing civilian clothing.

We understood that Sergeant Roche was a particularly active Crimes Special man, and his gloating over the corpse of Treacy had irritated even some of his own associates.

D.I. O'Sullivan of the R.I.C. was employed by the British in a clerical capacity. He had made the acquaintance of a lady employed in Messrs. Arnott's, and she subsequently became his fiancée. While waiting for her coming from business in Henry St. he was shot on the 12th December 1920, by members of the squad on instructions from Intelligence Office.

Through information received through one of our contacts employed as a waiter in the Wicklow Hotel, it was confirmed that Doran, the night porter, was in contact with enemy Intelligence officers during curfew hours, and instructions were received that he was to be liquidated. Several efforts were made to carry the order into effect and on 28th January 1921, our contact in the hotel, Paddy O'Shea, raised the restaurant blind, indicating that the man then leaving the hotel was Doran. Doran walked in the direction of some of the waiting squad who acted on my signal and shot him. Subsequently Doran's widow communicated to Michael Collins that her husband had been shot by Crown forces and that she was in dire straits financially. Rather than tell her the true facts, Collins instructed that she receive financial assistance.

Arising out of a letter which had been intercepted in the course of post by one of Collins's sorters, the location of the writer, Captain Cecil Lees, was discovered. Captain Lees had not been in Dublin very long when he wrote the letter (reproduced in facsimile in Piaras Beaslai's 'Michael Collins') to a friend of his in the War Office, indicating that he had been in touch with Major S.S. Hill Dillon, District G.S.O., Intelligence Branch, Dublin District, Royal Barracks. From the nature of the text it was clear that Captain Lees was a British Secret Service Agent engaged in the preliminary surveying of prospects for the murder of Irish leaders. This communication was sent to the Director of Intelligence for his instructions and was returned with the comment: '"Oggs" him'. This was the code word for the immediate execution of Captain Lees. I and other Intelligence officers, with members of the squad, took up positions each morning endeavouring to intercept Lees leaving his hotel, and on one such morning when he left at an early hour, I think about nine o'clock, he was shot on his way to the Castle.

Brady and Halpin were shot on 4th June 1921 by members of F/Company, 2nd Battalion, under the command of Lieutenant Danny Lyons. They had been acting as touts in conveying information to the Crown forces. The information relative to their activities had been supplied through the Brigade Intelligence officers.

Robert Pike was shot on 18th June 1921. He was a member of the tinker class and lived in Tolka Cottages, Drumcondra. I believe he was an ex-soldier who had been in the world war, and he was conveying information to the Crown forces. There was an unconfirmed statement that he had reported on Dan Breen's and Sean Treacy's movements from Fleming's of Drumcondra to Fernside.

Appleford and Bennett were two Auxiliary cadets of F/Company and were shot in Grafton St. in an abortive encircling movement on 24th June 1921. It was intended to enclose Grafton St. and shoot any members of the Crown forces who happened to be there. These two individual cadets, Appleford and Bennett, had been recognised by the Intelligence present, from a marked photograph of F/Company of the Auxiliaries which had been supplied to the Intelligence Department by Sergeant Reynolds, already referred to. The general intention was that anyone in Grafton St. who was fashionably dressed and believed to be an enemy agent was to be shot.

The Director of Intelligence received a report from a veterinary student, Sean Hyde, who was living in 20 Lower Mount St., to the effect that there were two suspects by the names of McMahon and Anglis, living in No. 21

Lower Mount St., where a number of medical students were lodging. I was instructed to investigate and I met Hyde, who gave me all the facts. It would appear that one of these men, McMahon, had been out during curfew on the night that Mr. Lynch of Kilmallock had been shot by Crown forces in the Exchange Hotel, Parliament St. These suspects did not go out in the daytime except to an ex-servicemen's club, known as the South Irish Horse Club, in Merrion Square. They also occasionally visited a billiards saloon at the rear of a tobacconist shop in Mount St. This was owned by a Mr. Kerr who was not sympathetic to the movement.

I duly reported back, and instructions were issued that these men were to be shot if they could be intercepted on the street. I was working on this assignment with some members of the Squad, on some occasions with Tom Keogh, Joe Leonard and others. We were unsuccessful in sighting the wanted men. One of Hyde's friends reported one evening that the two men had gone into Kerr's billiards saloon. On this occasion I was accompanied only by Joe Leonard. We went into the saloon, in which there was one table, and two gentlemen were playing billiards. The only description I had of McMahon, who was the principal party, was that he wore a signet ring on a finger of his left hand. We sat down on the seat and decided that when the man who was wearing the ring came to our side of the table we would fire. While thus engaged, preparatory to taking action, Hyde's friend, Conny O'Leary, rushed in and said that McMahon had gone back into his house.

On a check-up afterwards, it appeared that while McMahon had, in fact, entered the shop, he had gone to an upstairs apartment to see a girl, and was not the individual we had seen in the billiards saloon.

We continued after McMahon for a day or two, but the Director of Intelligence deferred action in view of reports which had come to hand concerning the location of other suspects residing in various parts of the city.

THE RE-ARMAMENT OF THE VOLUNTEERS AFTER 1916.

When I joined the Volunteers there were very few arms held by members of the Dublin Brigade, and it became one of our regular duties to report on and seize arms either at private houses or from government sources when opportunity arose.

After the first shooting activities by the Volunteers, it was discovered that a source of supply, viz: serving Tommies, for ammunition was being exploited by the Castle authorities for the issuing surreptitiously of explosive revolver ammunition to Volunteers. Fortunately, information of this move was received, and a general warning was issued to all Volunteers to examine their .45

revolver ammunition for any rounds which bore an imprint 'Z.Z.' as these were explosive cartridges.

In addition to these activities, I participated in many actions, including the seizure of arms from Messrs Guinness's boat 'the Clarecastle', the filling of home-made hand grenades with gelignite, the attempted shooting of hangmen on arrival at Dublin to carry out executions, attempted rescues of prisoners in military custody (Barton, the T.D., at Blessington St., and Dan Breen from the Mater Hospital, after being wounded at Fernside), and the encirclement of Grafton St. shortly before the Truce.

SPECIAL MISSION TO LONDON.

Before I was actually attached to the Intelligence Department, but in the period during which I had carried out a few jobs with the brigade or squad, the brigadier sent for me and I met him at 44 or 46 Parnell Square. Several other Volunteers selected from the different companies were there also, but Dick McKee and Peadar Clancy interviewed us individually. I was asked had I ever been to London, and I said I had not. I was then asked would I be prepared to go there on a special mission and I said 'certainly'. I was told to be available to travel at short notice, but no further instructions were received about this, so I did not make the trip across.

It was stated afterwards that the object of this visit

to London was the shooting of members of the British Cabinet, at the instigation of the Minister for Defence, Cathal Brugha. From stories I heard subsequently, it would appear that the Director of Intelligence, Michael Collins, opposed the plan as being as impracticable and out of harmony with his own plans.

RAIDS ON MAILS.

The first of these was the seizure of the Castle mails at Lower Dominick St., en route to the Castle from the Rink. This raid was carried out by the squad under Mick McDonnell's command. In the party were Tom Keogh, Jim Slattery, Vinnie Byrne and myself; there may have been one or two others, but I cannot recollect them.

The next raid was on the chief sorting office in the Rink, and was carried out by a party of Volunteers selected by the Vice-Commandant of the 2nd Battalion, Oscar Traynor. As it took place immediately before I joined the Intelligence Staff, I was acting under the command of Traynor on that occasion.

I was in the first party to approach the Rink, and entered the building by going down the mail chutes for the bags. Joe Dolan and another Intelligence Officer had already entered the building and joined our party in holding up the postal staff.

This raid was made possible by the information and

maps supplied by one of our contacts, Patrick Moynihan (118), indicating the layout of the Rink and the section where the Government mails were sorted and held.

It is interesting to note that an armoured car always accompanied the mails in transit, and that the building was equipped with alarm bells direct to the Castle. Fortunately, the raid was carried out with such swiftness that we were able to frustrate any attempt to give an alarm, and all government mails for the various Departments were successfully seized. These included mails for the R.I.C., Under-Secretary, Viceroy, military, etc.

The third raid was on Ballsbridge post office. While operating with the Intelligence Department, we received a report that the newly-formed Auxiliary Division with their headquarters at Beggars Bush Barracks, sent a tender of Cadets each morning at about nine o'clock to collect their mails at Ballsbridge post office.

Having surveyed the collections, I submitted a report which was transferred to the Brigadier for local action, and a successful seizure of the Auxiliaries' mails was made.

The knowledge gained through captured documents was of great value to us. Not alone was the information thus obtained of military importance, but the fact that the transmission of mails became unreliable deterred many would-be informers from sending information through the post.

As a matter of interest, the addresses obtained from the private correspondence of Auxiliary Cadets helped to establish the identity of these people, together with their home addresses in Great Britain. After the burning and sacking of Irish towns, reprisals were taken by the I.R.A. in Great Britain by burning some of the Cadets' homes.

Arising out of the initial shootings and raids for mails, large sums were offered by way of rewards to the people of Dublin for information which would lead to the arrest of the participants.

ATTEMPTED RESCUE OF ROBERT BARTON, T.D., AT BERKELEY ROAD.

On 12th February 1920, on instructions from the brigadier, we took up positions at the junction of Mountjoy St., Berkeley Road and Nelson St. We had been advised that Barton, who was on trial in the Dublin police courts, would be removed to Mountjoy jail in a military van.

When the military van was approaching, some of the Volunteers present ran out a handcart containing painter's ladders, thus stopping the progress of the van. We drew our pistols and surrounded the van. In the excitement one of the Volunteers discharged his revolver, wounding himself in the leg. However, Barton was not with the party in the van, and as they were unarmed, they were allowed to proceed on their way. Major C[a]rew was in charge of

the British party, and appealed to us not to lose our heads
and shoot them.

PLAN FOR THE WIPING OUT OF THE POLITICAL BRANCH OF 'G' DIVISION IN ONE ACTION.

In September 1920, before becoming a whole-time member
of the Intelligence Department, when I was assisting the
squad, I was instructed to accompany Paddy Daly and Joe
Leonard and report with other members of the squad for
an operation to be carried out outside the Upper Castle
Yard in the maze of alley-ways that approached the rear
entrance of to [*sic*] S.S. Michael and John's Church.

We took up the various positions indicated by Mick
McDonnell, and we were advised that a party of the
political branch of 'G' Division would leave from the
Upper Castle Yard on their way to eight o'clock Mass in
the church mentioned, as was their habit. This was the
only occasion that these much-wanted men left the Castle
during the week.

Tom Cullen, who was the Assistant Director of Intelligence, took up a position quite close to the Castle Gate,
and on a signal from him the job was to proceed. The reason that this signal was necessary before action taking place
was to safeguard McNamara should he be a member of the
party leaving the Castle, as happened. On the first occasion
the job was abortive for this reason. Each subsequent Sun-

day we took up positions, but the job was called off on the spot, due to the fact that Terry McSwiney was not dead. The latter had been on hunger-strike for a lengthy period, and Collins deferred action until such time as McSwiney would die, so that this would be a fitting climax. In all, we took up positions on four or five Sundays.

BRITISH MILITARY FIRED ON AT NEWCOMEN BRIDGE.

On a Sunday morning early in the month of October 1920, accompanied by Joe Leonard of the squad, we called to collect Paddy Daly at his residence, Bessboro' Avenue, North Strand, shortly after curfew had ended. We were proceeding shortly after 7 o'clock to report to Michael McDonnell at Saints Michael and John's in connection with the attempted ambush of members of the political branch of the 'G' Division.

Approaching Newcomen Bridge, a lorry containing British Tommies passed us by and pulled up on the Canal Bridge, the soldiers taking up positions on the bridge for search and hold-up purposes. The three of us turned sharply at left angles down Ossory Road where we crossed a wall on to the railway lines. We took Daly's gun from him and he proceeded to join the squad at its rendezvous, having to pass through the military picket. As daylight broke, we saw a sergeant and some soldiers walking down the railway in our direction, so we decamped and proceeded along the link-line towards Drumcondra. From each overhead bridge we could see a military party on each corresponding canal bridge. At 8.30 a.m., which was approximately the time the squad would be returning, we decided to fire on the military holding Binn's Bridge, Drumcondra. We both emptied our pistols – I was using a mauser (a peter-the-painter) and Leonard, a colt (.45), and we saw two soldiers fall as a result of our fire. The range was approximately 200 yards. We proceeded along the railway for about a quarter of a mile and climbed down on to the roadway in the neighbourhood of my house. We continued along to Botanic Avenue to the house of a Volunteer Goggins where we left our arms.

As a result of the unexpected attack, the military cordon was withdrawn from all canal bridges and the roads left free again.

Subsequently, Brigadier McKee sent for me and asked me what was in my mind in firing on the soldiers. He seemed to be satisfied with the explanation I gave him. Shortly afterwards, this action was cited in 'An t-Oglach' as a splendid example of initiative and, as far as I know, this was the first occasion on which British military had been fired on since the Insurrection. Following this incident the policy of the I.R.A. was extended so as to include attacks on armed soldiers in addition to police and enemy agents.

SWOOP ON ENEMY AGENTS ON 21ST NOVEMBER 1920.

I was instructed by the Deputy Director of Intelligence to contact a girl who had reported to a Volunteer about some strange residents who were occupying the block of flats in which she was a maid. I met her in this Volunteer's home over a shop in Talbot St. I think his name was Byrne. I questioned the girl, whose name was Maudie. She described the routine of the residents of the flats, and it would seem from her account that they followed no regular occupation but did a lot of office work in their flats. I arranged with her to bring me the contents of the waste-paper baskets. When these were examined we found torn up documents which referred to the movements of wanted Volunteers, and also photographs of wanted men.

The D.I. and G.H.Q. staff then decided, in the light of Intelligence reports supplied, that the only certain method of dealing with these enemy agents was by surprise and general attack, rather than by picking them off individually.

I last met Maudie on the Saturday evening, 20th November 1920, at our rendezvous, and she told me that all her 'boarders' were at home, with the exception of two who were changing their residence that night to Upper Mount Street. I duly reported to the Brigade Headquarters and told Dick McKee of the change of address of two of them and he had already briefed all the squads for action on the following morning. However, he made up a patch unit to attend to the officers in Upper Mount Street.

On the Saturday night I stopped as usual in the 'dugout' where we used to stay while on the run. This was located in the unoccupied portion of Summerhill Dispensary, and we gave accommodation for the night to several other Volunteers who were going into action in the morning.

Before curfew that night, I left the Brigade office in the Plaza in Gardiner's Row and proceeded to Harcourt St. to meet the officer who would accompany me to 28 and 29 Upper Pembroke St. on the following morning. It was thus that I met Paddy Flanagan of the 3rd Battalion, and we fixed a rendezvous for the morning.

When I arrived at Upper Pembroke St. on the Sunday morning, I met Flanagan and a few other Volunteers. I explained to Flanagan that we had no keys for the hall doors in order to gain admission, so we went over our arrangements.

Fortunately, at the zero hour of 9 a.m., the hall door was open and the porter was shaking mats on the steps. There were separate staircases in this double house and a party proceeded up either staircase to the rooms already indicated. I accompanied Flanagan and two other Volunteers to a room at the top of the house occupied by two officers, one of these being Lieut. Dowling. We knocked at the door and pushed it open. The two officers were awake in bed. They were told to stand up and were then shot.

I told Flanagan that I wanted to search the room and he said: 'Search be damned! Get out of here'. We proceeded down the staircase to the hallway, where a number of other officers had been rounded up from their rooms and were lined up against the side of the staircase that led in the direction of the basement. Our reaching this level was the signal for a volley.

In all there were six or seven agents in residence at this address, all holding British military commissions. All of them were shot, but a few survived their wounds.

All the papers that were captured that morning were brought to Mrs. Byrne's house in North Richmond St. and were later conveyed by me to our office in Crow Street.

Although instructions were issued for about twenty different operations on the Sunday morning, several were not carried out. Later on, reports were supplied by our officers and these were examined and filed in the Intelligence Office. In some instances the excuses put forward for the non-carrying out of instructions were not considered very satisfactory; in particular, those received from the Commandant of the 1st Battalion regarding two addresses they should have visited on the North Circular Road, adjacent to the Phoenix Park.

The effect of this swoop was very marked, inasmuch as Detective McNamara told me that scenes never before witnessed took place in the Castle. Cabs, sidecars and all modes of conveyance brought people into the Castle who had been operating surreptitiously against the I.R.A.; they were driven in there by their consciences in order to secure protection. In this manner, the efficiency and the effectiveness of the British Secret Service in Ireland was brought to a standstill.

THE IGOE SQUAD.

Towards the end of 1920 a young Irish Volunteer officer by the name of Howlett, who had arrived at Broadstone railway station from the west, was waylaid and shot dead by men dressed in civilian clothes. It was inferred by the Castle authorities that this shooting was done by Sinn Fein elements.

In our investigations which followed, the name Igoe was mentioned for the first time in our Intelligence Office and inquiries were set afoot to identify him, as he and some of his associates had shot Howlett.

A report was received to the effect that several country members of the R.I.C. were living in the Depot, Phoenix Park, and were moving around the city in civilian clothes.

We had no lead to begin inquiries until I was instructed to interview a lady who ran a tea-room and was a member of Cumann na mBan. I made the acquaintance of this lady, Miss Maire Gleeson, the proprietress of the West End Cafe, Parkgate St. This was located adjacent to the main entrance to Phoenix Park, and was a small shop with a tea-rooms [*sic*] attached. Miss Gleeson informed me that amongst her patrons were several plain-clothes R.I.C. men who dropped in shortly before curfew for a light supper fairly frequently. She said they were living in the Depot. From further investigations it was clear that Head Constable Igoe and other members of his party were the diners mentioned by Miss Gleeson.

I duly reported the facts and the Director of Intelligence had active inquiries made through Brigade Intelligence Officers throughout the country as to the absence from their home stations of the constabulary who were engaged on political work.

In retrospect it would appear that some – probably about a dozen – members of the R.I.C. who had become obnoxious in their own areas, through their zeal in tracking down Volunteers, had been transferred to the Depot for special work, and were acting under the instructions of Head Constable Igoe. These men were ideally situated to carry out the task allotted to them, which was evidently the tracking down of country Volunteers visiting the city, and summarily shooting them. In other respects they were invaluable to General Tudor, the officer commanding the

Auxiliary Division of the R.I.C., and to the headquarters staff who were dealing with political information from the country, inasmuch as their services were available for identification purposes in connection with reports reaching the Depot from the country. As time passed, inter-communication between Dublin and the Provinces through the official channels became more hazardous, and the advantage of having men on the spot with a knowledge of their respective local situations was a great asset to the Crown forces.

I met Miss Gleeson several times, but the information obtained was insufficient for an ambush to be arranged. Although efforts were made many times in this connection, the movements of these men were so erratic that no results could be obtained.

In January 1921, the Director of Intelligence had transferred to Dublin a Volunteer by the name of Thomas Newell (also known as Sweeney Newell) who knew Igoe personally, and Newell was attached to our Department in an external capacity.

About this time Igoe and his squad had adopted a technique of moving as a patrol through the streets of Dublin in a formation that was not noticeable to the pedestrians, and if they came across any country Volunteers in their strolls they either arrested them or beat them up and then arrested them. Needless to remark, as street activities became more general, this patrol became a menace to the Dublin Volunteers who were moving around the streets carrying out ambushes or other jobs.

On a weekday in January, Newell rushed in to our office in Crow St. at about eleven o'clock in the morning and stated that he had seen Igoe and his party proceeding up Grafton St. in the direction of St. Stephen's Green. I immediately accompanied Newell, and, simultaneously, instructions were sent to the squad, who were 'standing by' in the headquarters in Upper Abbey St., to assemble at St. Stephen's Green and await instructions from me.

As Igoe had been in the habit of visiting railway stations, I assumed that he was heading for Harcourt Street station and that should this be so we could manoeuvre our squad into action positions on St. Stephen's Green, West, to ambush Igoe's party on their return journey.

Newell and I proceeded to Grafton St. by the shortest route, and when we had almost reached Weir's jewellery stores in Grafton Street, I noticed that we had been passed by some men, who, I instinctively recognised as Igoe's party, altho' Newell had not had time to confirm this. When they had passed us out, they wheeled on us, and at close range said: 'Don't move', which we did not, as we were unarmed. This manoeuvre took place with pedestrians passing by, unaware of anything unusual taking place.

Without much delay, we were told to keep walking, and

a surrounding formation of Igoe's squad kept pace with us as well as accompanying us.

We walked, as directed, up Suffolk St. and down Trinity St. until we came to a building in Dame St. (No. 38) which was an insurance office, where we were directed to stand against the wall. Newell was kept several paces away from me, and we were surrounded by a bodyguard on either side. I should mention that Newell was dressed in typical country fashion. He was wearing a cap and greatcoat, and was easily identifiable as a man from the country.

Igoe, whom I had identified from his description, first questioned Newell and later questioned me, but neither of us could hear the other's answers.

While in this predicament, I saw Vincent Byrne and other members of the squad cutting across Dame St. and going through Hely's Arch, on their way to St. Stephen's Green to the rendezvous. They evidently thought that I was engaged in conversation with some friends, as they made no effort to approach us.

In reply to the questions put to me, I gave my correct name and address. I stated that I was a believer in Home Rule and that my father was a J.P. and did not agree with the Sinn Fein policy.

Newell endeavoured to bluff also, and we were asked how we came to know one another. I stated that he was a stranger I had met on the street who had got into conversation with me and that I was directing him somewhere or other. I failed to realise at the time that Igoe was aware of Newell's position in the Galway Volunteers and knew him quite well. Under the interrogation Newell lost his temper and told Igoe that he knew who he was, just as well as Igoe knew him. His outburst ended any further questioning.

I was told to walk on and not look back. I walked on in the direction of Trinity St., knowing from the footsteps behind me that I was under cover by some of Igoe's men. I moved fairly slowly at first, not being physically able to go any faster. I moved through Trinity St., Suffolk St. and into Wicklow St., gaining a few yards on each bend and keeping civilians, as far as possible, in the line of fire between myself and my pursuers.

When I turned the corner of Wicklow St. I made a dash of about thirty or forty yards and entered a building where my father had his commercial offices. I went up the two flights of stairs into his office and was practically in a state of collapse on reaching it. My father's typist was in the office, but I did not speak to her as I expected to hear the sound of steps on the stairs any second. After about five minutes, as nothing happened, I asked her to put on her hat and coat and accompany me, which she did. We walked out from the office and cut up Clarendon St. as far as St. Stephen's Green, where I parted with my pilot and located the squad.

Having told Tom Keogh what happened, I got hold of

a gun and we all returned to Dame St. in the hope of over-taking some of Igoe's party. We searched several streets in the area without coming across them. We assumed that they must have entered the Castle, as they were nowhere to be seen.

Our surmise proved to be somewhat correct. Although Newell was not brought into the Castle, some of Igoe's men went in and secured motor cars. Newell was brought – I think he was walked – to Greek St. adjacent to the Bridewell, where he was riddled and thrown into a car and driven to King George V Hospital. His wounds did not prove fatal, however, but before receiving medical aid his legs, which had been broken by bullets, were twisted in an effort to get information from him. He was detained in custody, and was one of the first prisoners claimed by Michael Collins on the signing of the Treaty.

Subsequently, an all-out effort was made, not alone by the Active Service Unit, but by all units that were available in the Dublin Brigade, to shoot Igoe and his party. Many abortive attempts were made, without the desired effect. Possibly Igoe became more cautious, because they used Ford cars for their excursions between the Depot and the Castle, and did not move around on foot except on very rare occasions.

The personnel of Igoe's party was never fully established, beyond the fact that it contained members from the different 'hot spots' in the country. They were all Irishmen who had considerable service in the R.I.C., with the exception of a Scotsman who was known as Jock. He may have become associated through his membership of the Black and Tans. Due to the fact that he had committed some crime, they did not want him to appear in police uniform.

Igoe's party were effective in their duties, and picked up a number of Volunteers, many of whom, fortunately, were imprisoned. This party became one of the most difficult and dangerous forces opposed to the I.R.A. in Dublin.

VINCENT FOUVARGE AND BRIGADE INTELLIGENCE.

Later on, the Brigade Intelligence Service was organised by the appointment of an Intelligence Officer to each Company in the Brigade. These, in turn, operated through a Battalion Intelligence Officer, who then reported to the Brigade Intelligence Officer. None of these men were whole time on the Intelligence Staff, and only operated on Intelligence as part of their Volunteer duties.

The first Brigade I.O. was Peter Ennis.

1st Battalion I.O. – Tom Walsh.

2nd Battalion I.O. –

3rd Battalion I.O. –

4th Battalion I.O. – Vincent Fouvarge.

During the course of a Crown forces raid, Fouvarge was arrested. He was questioned and released. It would appear that while in captivity he divulged information regarding his I.R.A. duties and associations. Fouvarge left Dublin for London and was shot on a golf course by Sam Maguire or his men, on the instructions of the Director of Intelligence.

Arising out of that incident, Peter Ennis was arrested by Captain Hardy and company and received inhuman treatment in the Castle, all his teeth being kicked out. It was believed that there was a connection between Ennis's arrest and Fouvarge's information.

ATTEMPTED LARGE-SCALE AMBUSH OF 'F' COY., AUXILIARIES.

A large party of specially picked Volunteers from the 2nd Battalion, under Sean Russell and Tom Ennis, took up positions one night on the Great Northern railway bridge which runs across Seville Place. I was in the party and there was a Volunteer from 'E' Company, 2nd Battalion, who worked in the shipyards, and he had invented a super bomb. This was constructed with a large outer case containing rivets, and must have weighed several stone. The intention was to drop this bomb from the bridge into the street at the opportune moment.

The plan of operation was that my colleague, Tom

Cullen, Assistant D.I., would ring Dublin Castle from a house in Seville Place, and inform them that the Battalion headquarters was full of Volunteers. The house selected to telephone from was that of a Unionist, adjacent to 100 Seville Place, which was Battalion Headquarters.

It was assumed that on receipt of the message by Dublin Castle authorities, they would send several tenders of Auxiliaries to raid the hall. Although in position for almost an hour, no raid was made by the authorities on the hall, but a convoy of Auxiliaries with armoured cars passed along Amiens St. from the Castle and proceeded out to Killester, where they raided Furry Park, the residence of a friend of Michael Collins.

From inquiries made later, an unconfirmed report stated that the Castle authorities 'phoned the nearest D.M.P. Bks and instructed them to send a D.M.P. man to find out if the building was occupied, and that when he arrived he found it in total darkness and no sign of life within. On the other hand, it may have been that all their available forces were already detailed for the raid which was carried out at Killester about the same hour.

SECRET MEETINGS OF DÁIL ÉIREANN.

One such meeting was convened and held at Alderman Cole's house in Mountjoy Square, at which, I believe, important decisions were made regarding the progress of the war. Only those members who were not in jail or interned attended and, as most of these were Volunteer officers, and more particularly, because Michael Collins, Cathal Brugha and Dick McKee were attending, myself and a few other members of the Intelligence Department performed security guard duties at the house to deal with any attempted raid by Crown forces.

On another occasion we took up similar protective duty outside the residence of Professor O'Rahilly in Herbert Park where Michael Collins and members of the headquarters staff of the I.R.A. were meeting de Valera after his return from America.

CAPTURE OF ARMOURED CAR.

In late April 1921 I was instructed one evening by the Assistant Director of Intelligence to report to the Plaza Hotel in Gardiner's Row. This building was being used as the offices of a Trade Union body, and one of the offices was now our brigade headquarters. When I walked into the room I saw several staff officers assembled. Among them was the Director of Intelligence, Michael Collins. I knew Michael by sight, but this was the first occasion on which I met him face to face. He was sitting at a table, and he gave me a friendly nod when I reported to him. I felt very important to be in such company, but at the same time the presence of Michael completely overawed me. I was very vexed with myself not to be able to be at my ease, as I was most anxious to make a good impression.

He told me that the Superintendent of the Corporation abattoir (who was also a Volunteer officer) had reported to him that an armoured car called to the abbatoir [*sic*] each morning at six o'clock to escort supplies of meat to the military barracks. 'I want you to go to the Superintendent's house,' he said, 'and observe the movements of the crew and see if there is any possibility of capturing the car'.

Sean MacEoin was a prisoner in Mountjoy Jail. He was a fine and chivalrous soldier, having conducted the campaign in Longford with brilliant success and great humanity; but he had been captured after an ambush and was awaiting his courtmartial at which he was certain to be hanged. Michael Collins was determined to rescue him and, with the help of an armoured car, there was a chance. I was to take up residence in the Superintendent's house, and to make my observations over several mornings.

The next night, shortly before curfew, I went to the house. The Superintendent's wife, Mrs. Lynch, was expecting me. Her husband, the Volunteer, was 'on the run' and very much wanted by the Authorities, so that he was unable to sleep at home. The house was raided for him from time to time, which added to the precariousness of my position.

It was moonlight, and, while paying due attention

to what Mrs. Lynch was telling me, my eyes wandered round looking for a possible way of escape in the event of a raid on the house. To my horror I saw something else – a sight calculated to strike far greater fear to my soul than the approach of any number of armed men. Below me, scurrying about in the moonlight, were shoals of rats! I withdrew hastily from the window, making up my mind that, if that were my only way out, I would cheerfully allow myself to be murdered in my bed.

I was then shown to my room which looked most comfortable and inviting, and, after an excellent supper, I retired for the night. Mrs. Lynch promised to call me in good time so that I could watch the arrival of the armoured car in the morning. She was as good as her word, and, hurriedly dressing myself, I went down and took up my position by the drawing-room window. Kneeling down, I could see, through the lace fringe at the bottom of the blind, all that was going on. I saw the arrival of the armoured car. It accompanied two lorries and, while it pulled up exactly on the spot opposite the window, only a dozen paces away, which Mrs. Lynch had pointed out to me, the lorries were driven on up the yard to be loaded with the meat.

I saw the door of the car opened. Four soldiers got out. They were dressed in dungarees and each had a revolver on the holster of his belt. Lighting cigarettes, they stood chatting. It was a double-turreted car, and I knew the crew consisted of six men. On getting out, one of the soldiers had locked in the other two by fastening a small padlock on the door.

Morning after morning at six o'clock I took up my position behind the window and saw this performance repeated. The lorries, conducted by the armoured car, made several journeys with their cargoes of meat to and from the various barracks. While they were away I had my breakfast and made friends with the two children of whom I had grown very fond.

Every morning I made my observations and every day I reported them to Liam.

After a week I was summoned to another meeting at brigade headquarters. On this occasion we met at Barry's Hotel, a few doors from the Plaza, where to my surprise, and gratification, I again saw Michael Collins.

We sat around a table. Michael asked me to tell him what I had seen and what my opinion was in view of my observations.

I described the arrival of the car, the several journeys it made, and the conduct of the crew. I produced a sketch of my own, showing the position usually occupied by the car when in the abattoir. They heard me out without interruption. When I had finished, Michael Collins addressed me:

'I take it from your report you consider it possible to capture the car?'.

'I do, Sir,' said I, 'but our success depends upon the exact arrival of our men at the opportune moment, which may only occur very occasionally'.

I had already explained to the meeting that during the dozen or so times I had had the car under observation, only on one occasion did the whole crew leave it. Until such another occasion arose we could not capture it. When it did arise, it would be necessary for our men to be at hand to seize it instantly. This seemed to satisfy Michael.

'Since they left it once, they will probably do so again', he said.

He then addressed the others in turn. He first questioned Pat McCrea. Pat is a Co. Wicklow man, about forty years of age, an older man than most of us. He was out in the Larkin Strike and took part in the Rising, and was always to be found wherever there was any hard fighting to be done. Of a gentle disposition and charming manner, he endeared himself to everyone who ever had the pleasure of serving with him. Meeting him, it would not occur to you that he was a soldier, on account of the mildness of his address. Only, if you were observant, you might notice a directness in his glance which corrected your impression of his entirely peaceful disposition. He was our crack driver and took part in practically every action in Dublin.

Another meeting of the key men was held the following night, when final arrangements were made and last instructions given.

I returned to my post behind the blind.

Our plans for concerted action were now complete. The Volunteers, who were to hold up the soldier and to seize the car, were to gather unostentatiously in the neighbourhood of the abattoir. One man was to lie concealed in a spot from which he could see the window of one of the rooms in the Superintendent's house. From my vantage point I was to watch for the first occasion when all six men would leave the car. When this occurred I was to give a signal – I would raise the blind in that room which was visible to the waiting Volunteer. The moment he saw the blind go up, he would signal to the others who would appear at once upon the scene of action.

All of us were in our respective positions on the following morning. But only four of the soldiers left the car and, greatly disappointed, I saw there was again no chance. As soon as the car had moved off, I slipped out by the back and, getting on my bicycle, I made my way to headquarters. The waiting Volunteers, seeing me depart, moved away, knowing the job was off for that morning.

On the next morning, 14th May 1921, we made a slight change in our plans.

As usual, I was at my observation post at 6 a.m. When

the car arrived I formed the opinion that the crew were in a not over-zealous mood. They seemed to be less vigilant. That was my impression.

As soon as they drove off escorting the first delivery of meat, I made my way on my bicycle to a stable in Abbey St. which was used as a rendezvous and place of waiting by the Active Service Unit.

Here were assembled all the men on the job waiting for my message. Michael Collins was with them and I made my report.

MacEoin's days were now numbered, and Michael, fretted by the continual delays and disappointments, was most anxious that the attempt should be made at once. I told him I was optimistic and thought there would be a chance later in the morning when the armoured car returned. I based my hopes on that appearance of carelessness in the mood of the crew. Hurrying back to the house, once more I took up my position behind the blind. I was not long there when I saw the car return. It drew up outside the window. I saw four of the crew get out and wander away through the slaughter-houses. They had not locked the door of the car! I became excited and hopeful. With my eyes glued to the door, I wished with my whole being to see the remaining two soldiers step out. For a whole ten minutes I waited. Then I saw the door swing open. It had happened! I had got my wish!

On stepping out, they lit cigarettes, and one of them

shut the door, locking the padlock and putting the key in his pocket.

Nearly suffocating with excitement, I rushed into the room from which my signal was to be given and I raised the blind.

That was the most awful decision I have ever had to make. Those few moments were the longest of my life, while I waited to see the approach of our men up the avenue which led to the abattoir. From that window I could not see the car. It was possible that during those two minutes the soldiers had got in again and I would see the massacre of my comrades, men whose places could never be filled, and feel myself responsible for their loss.

While I waited, I shouted to Mrs. Lynch to get the children out of the way. We had arranged together that she should take them to a back bedroom, where they would be safe from stray bullets in the event of any firing.

Then I saw two Volunteers pass by the window. I recognised Tom Keogh. Dashing back to my post of observation at the other window, I was in time to see the two soldiers with their hands up, while our men were taking their revolvers. All my anxiety was over now. I was full of joy and relief.

The other Volunteers were scattering through the buildings, searching for the rest of the crew, who had gone to watch the animals being slaughtered.

Our men were getting ready to take over the armoured car. From my window I watched Pat McCrea, with a benign expression on his face, struggling to get his legs into a pair of dungarees. The other members of our crew were doing the same, while the soldiers were kept covered. They had brought dungarees in parcels, ready. They were dressing up for their new parts. I saw Pat take the cap off one of the Tommies and put it on his own head. It was too small for him. He jammed it on his head anyhow, so that it had a rakish look, while he still struggled to get his foot out through the leg of the dungarees. I found myself laughing as I watched him, and I waited to see him search the soldiers for the key of the padlock and, finding it, unlock the door of the car.

I had now seen enough. I ran upstairs to Mrs. Lynch. I told her the good news. Then I locked her and the children into one of the bedrooms, so that when the authorities arrived and the house was searched, she would not be suspected of any complicity, but would appear to be but one more of our victims.

At that moment I heard several shots ring out. It was necessary to be off. Jumping on my bicycle I hurried to the house where Joe and Emmet were waiting. It was round the corner in the North Circular Road. They were ready, dressed in the British uniforms. I had just time to notice that they looked very well in them.

'Come on', said I, still breathless with excitement, 'the car will be along any minute'.

They came out into the street. At the same moment the car appeared. We saw it turning out of the avenue and coming towards us. I saw Emmet and Joe picked up, and then, the happiest young man in Dublin that morning, I cycled away to the stable in Abbey St. There I found Michael Collins waiting. His look searched mine for an answer to the question there was no need to ask. He was overjoyed, and my satisfaction was unbounded to be the bearer of such good news to him. He was all smiles. 'I hope the second part will be as successful', he said.

AMBUSH OF BRITISH TROOPS AT DRUMCONDRA, 16TH JUNE 1921.

I accompanied a party from the squad and the A.S.U. in an endeavour to ambush a train containing newly-arrived troops in Ireland, en route to the Curragh.

This ambush was arranged to take place after many of the active Volunteers had been rounded up at the Custom House burning, and an all-out effort was being made by those still at liberty to increase the number of attacks, so that the enemy would not be aware of the depletion the Custom House arrests had made in the ranks of the active Volunteers in Dublin.

We took up positions along the roadway adjoining the

railway embankment adjacent to Lindsay Road, and myself and another Volunteer, with a Thompson gun each, took up position in a laneway covering the railway line adjacent to St. Columba's Road, Upper.

The party armed with grenades bombed the train before it came to our position. My companion opened fire with his gun, but I did not get my gun into action as the target only presented itself for about one minute. Neither of us had ever handled a Thompson gun before this. As a result of the fire, several soldiers were wounded. The train continued on its course, and the attackers decamped.

This was the first occasion on which the two Thompson sub-machine guns that were in the country were brought into action. It may not be irrelevant to mention that two American ex-officers of Irish descent had come to Ireland to offer their fighting services to Collins. Their names were Dineen and Cronin. Before this train ambush, they had demonstrated the Thompson guns, of which two had been successfully smuggled into the country, at the Casino, Malahide Road, to Michael Collins and some of his associates, but I was not personally present on this occasion and had not seen the gun in action before the train ambush. I was not given any instructions on the handling and loading of the Thompson machine guns. The two guns were brought to the rendezvous in a van, and myself and the other gunner were handed one each, which we had to keep concealed under our coats until the train came into view. However, I later made myself familiar with its mechanism, and carried one in the encircling movement of Grafton St. later on.

EFFORTS TO PREVENT HANGINGS AT MOUNTJOY.

On three or four occasions a number of Volunteers had been hanged in Mountjoy Jail by the public hangman, who crossed from England to carry out the executions. On each occasion an effort was made to intercept the hangman before he reached the jail, but in no instance was this successful.

On one such occasion I was instructed to proceed to Kingstown, as a report had been received that Ellis, the hangman, and his assistant were to arrive there some days before the date fixed for the executions.

The squad had a van stored in a garage at the rear of Lower Fitzwilliam St. and a Volunteer named Paddy Kelly undertook to drive it. Kelly was living with other Volunteers at an address in South William St., and it was necessary for me to stay with him overnight, as curfew was imposed at an early hour and did not finish until five or six o'clock in the morning. We left South William St. immediately after curfew, or possibly before it ended, and proceeded to Lower Fitzwilliam St. where we took out the car and drove to Kingstown, where we met Jimmy Murray, 6th Battalion I.O. We waited at the pier head and watched those passengers who disembarked from the mail boat and proceeded to waiting cars to drive to town. We had a description of the hangman, but no passenger thus alighting resembled him.

The information which we had received was of the most meagre character, and subsequently it was ascertained that the hangman always arrived in Dublin several days before the executions, were [*sic*] taken to Mountjoy in an armoured car and left there under special protection.

ENCIRCLEMENT OF AREA IN DUBLIN BY CROWN FORCES.

In company with two members of the squad, Joe Leonard and Jimmy Conroy, I was staying on the run at night in the Summerhill Dispensary, having secured permission to do so from Relieving Officer Madden.

We were awakened one morning during curfew, and saw from our bedroom window large parties of military on the street. They were driving sticks into the ground and erecting barbed wire entanglements. We also saw tanks and armoured cars, and, guessing that there was something unusual afoot, we decided to vacate our quarters. While crossing the back wall into the laneway we saw a Tommy, but as his back was turned to us, he did not see us. We crossed further walls and got on to the roadway at the N.C. Road.

While proceeding along the N.C. Road towards Jones's Road three tenders of Auxiliaries passed. They did not see us, because, fortunately, a doorway opened and a postman inquired from us what hour it was. Leonard pushed him into the doorway and closed the door behind him; we scampered down a side road.

WHAT MICK McDONNELL ASKED ME TO RECORD.

Two years ago, Mick McDonnell was on a visit to this country from California, and he spent an evening with me discussing matters about which he said he would like me to have the correct facts. He also promised that, if an opportunity arose, he would give me a resumé of his complete activities in the movement, but, unfortunately, that never materialised, and it can never be done as he died recently.

Regarding the formation of the squad, Mick stated that a number of selected Volunteers were assembled at 42 North Great George's St. on the instructions of Dick McKee. These men, many of them with service in the 1916 insurrection, were informed by the brigadier that a certain line of action would be necessary if the movement was to continue. In this connection he indicated that it would be necessary to shoot some members of the 'G' Division whose political activities had jeopardised the activities of the re-formed Volunteers.

There were present three or four members of each of the five companies which then constituted the 2nd Battalion, and after the brigadier's address, most of those present refused to give an affirmative answer to the request made by him. Some of the men advanced the reason that they could not do such work as it would be contrary to their consciences; others stated that they would think the matter over and get spiritual advice before giving an answer, and, finally, some of them stated that, while they were prepared to carry out acts of open warfare, they were not prepared to shoot a man down unwarned. (The 'G' men had received several warnings before action was taken.)

Mick McDonnell told me that when the question was put to those present from 'E' Company, he stepped out of the ranks as also did Jim Slattery and, probably, Vincent Byrne and Tom Keogh.

I was discussing this matter subsequently with Jim Slattery and he confirmed Mick McDonnell's story and stated that he said to the brigadier: 'I am prepared to carry out any and every order I receive from you'.

Mick McDonnell told me that amongst the dissenters, for one reason or another, were Cyril Daly, Oscar Traynor

(?), I think, and Frank Kearney, all of 'F' Company, 2nd Battalion.

From my close association with the various members of the squad subsequently, I learned that in the initial stages a few jobs were carried out independently by Paddy Daly, Joe Leonard and Ben Barrett. At one period of the fighting, Paddy Daly was imprisoned as was also Joe Leonard. This would suggest that two squads operated in the early stages. Later on, the squad consisted of about twelve members. Paddy Daly, after his release from Ballykinlar, took charge of the newly-formed active service unit, while Joe Leonard continued in the squad.

During my association with the squad and previous to my joining the Intelligence Staff, Mick McDonnell was in charge of the operations I was concerned with, namely, the seizure of the mail van at Lower Dominick St. and the attempt to ambush 'G' men at SS. Michael and John's Church. Later on, when the squad had reached its full strength of about a dozen men, they stood-to for hours at Seville Place and other centres and acted on the instructions of the Deputy Director of Intelligence.

It might not be inapt to add in conclusion that throughout the whole period of active service in which I was associated with members of the squad and Intelligence and Volunteers in the city, I found that the morale was always very high and that everyone was anxious to do his part without any consideration as to personal danger or inconvenience and that a very strong spirit of comradeship resulted which, I am glad to say, survived in the years that followed.

SIGNED: CHARLES F. DALTON
DATE: 12TH OCTOBER 1950
WITNESS: W. IVORY. COMDT

Index